ROMANS
THE *Letter* THAT CHANGED THE WORLD

VOLUME I

by Hudson Productions
3405 Milton Ave., Suite 207
Dallas, TX 75205

Editor in Chief:
        Carrie Hudson
        Doug Hudson

All Scripture quotations are taken from
the Ryrie Study Bible, 1978 Edition
The New American Standard Translation
Moody Press, Chicago

Printed in the United States of America

Resources

ECCLESIASTES
A Life Well Lived (A Study of Ecclesiastes)
Bible Study Series by Tommy Nelson
      4 DVD Curriculum
      Companion Study Guide
      A Life Well Lived paperback book

LOVELIFE
NEW! Song of Solomon
Bible Study Series by Mark Driscoll
      4 DVD Curriculum
      Companion Study Guide
      Packages and bulk discounts available

DANIEL
Things to Come
Bible Study Series by Tommy Nelson
      4 DVD Curriculum
      Companion Study Guide
      Understand prophecy and how it can change your life

PHILIPPIANS
NEW! Philippians, To Live is Christ & to Die is Gain
Bible Study Series by Matt Chandler
      4 DVD Curriculum
      Companion Study Guide
      Packages and bulk discounts available

RUTH
NEW! Your God. My God. A True Story of Love & Redemption
Bible Study Series by Tommy Nelson
      4 DVD Curriculum
      Companion Study Guide
      Packages and bulk discounts available

SONG OF SOLOMON
NEW and Improved! 1995 Song of Solomon Classic
DVD Curriculum by Tommy Nelson
      Enhanced video, audio and color graphics
      Updated and enlarged companion Study Guide
      Formatted for Widescreen

NEW! Enhanced SOS for Students
DVD Curriculum by Tommy Nelson
      Re-Mastered Video & Audio
      All new graphics and menus
      Never before seen Q & A's
      All in one Study Guide for both Students & Leaders

VINTAGE JESUS
NEW! Vintage Jesus, Timeless Answers to Timely Questions
Bible Study Series by Mark Driscoll
      4 DVD Curriculum
      Companion Study Guide
      Packages and bulk discounts available

Acknowledgements

This project has been an honor to produce. Through this study, our prayer is that many will come to follow Christ. We would like to thank the following people, who helped to make this such a great success!

Tommy Nelson
Matt Coleman and Unblind Productions
Drew Rodgers at Livingstone Designs
Shatrine Krake and Simply Design
Our wonderful audience and their hours of dedication
Jason Countryman and Pocketpak

To God be the Glory! *Doug and Carrie Hudson*

About The Hub

Thanks for taking a moment to learn more about us. Our organization began in 1995 working with one speaker, Tommy Nelson and one amazing message, The Song of Solomon. It was and is our privilege to help champion God's written Word on Love, Dating, Marriage and Sex based directly on Song of Solomon. It is a book that has been censored for centuries and it has been a total blessing and thrill to see it change my life, and millions of others.

As of August 2009 we have rebranded our organization to reflect the root of our passion and the future of our organization:

To Develop, Find and Share life changing Bible Centric tools that move people forward. We have renamed our organization to The Hub. It is our passion and commitment to be a Hub for unique, challenging and grace filled resources. I hope you will agree after you participate and interact with one of our resources. God Bless you and know that if you will listen, God's Truth will move you forward in life, no matter where you have been or are currently.

Doug Hudson, President - The Hub

Table of Contents

Volume One

BEFORE YOU GO ANY FURTHER…READ THIS!

If you are a small group leader, thanks for taking the opportunity to shepherd others along the way. And if you are using this series for personal study, get ready for a life-changing experience you will want to share with others! Here are a few tips as you get started with the series:

• This study was designed with small groups in mind. So put a small group together and get started.
• The series is also perfect for individuals or couples who are looking for ways to deepen their devotions or find practical ways to apply the timeless truths of Scripture.
• Volume One is designed to be used as either a 12-week or a 6-week study. Each DVD session is 30 minutes long. The sessions are designed to be used as follows: watch each session and then discuss the questions in the study guide.
• Depending on the length of your meeting time, you can watch two sessions per meeting to make Volume One a 6-week series.
• Volume One covers Romans 1-8.

A WORD TO SMALL GROUP LEADERS

There is no separate leader's guide. Leaders are facilitators of the material: Answers to Text Questions are in the back of study guide.

Before each session we encourage leaders to:

• Pray – ask the Lord for guidance on how to lead the members in your group. Pray that He will show you ways to stimulate genuine, dynamic and open communication.
• Preview – it will be very beneficial for you to watch the session before you share it with your group. You will notice the key points from each session and you can better facilitate the discussion questions within your group.
• Prepare – a small group will only go as deep and be as transparent as the leader. If a leader or facilitator is not willing to get personal, then the group will float on the surface. Let God speak through your own struggles and weaknesses.

About the Speaker

Tommy Nelson has been the Pastor of Denton Bible Church, in Denton, Texas, since 1977.

Tommy graduated from the University of North Texas with a Bachelor's Degree in Education. He then attended Dallas Theological Seminary in Dallas, Texas, where he received the Master of Arts in Biblical Studies degree.

Tommy has been married to Teresa Nelson since 1974. They have two grown sons, Ben and John, along with five grand-children.

Other Tommy Nelson Bible Studies:
- Song of Solomon
- Song of Solomon - Student Series
- Ecclesiastes (A Life Well Lived)
- Daniel
- Romans, Volume II
- Ruth

PAUL'S ADDRESS TO THE ROMANS
Romans 1:1-17

In session one Paul begins his letter to move Jew and Gentile to faith in Jesus Christ. In this session he specifically addresses the Romans and tells them of his desire to be with them.

CHAPTER 1

¹Paul, a bond-servant of Christ Jesus, called as an apostle, set apart for the gospel of God,

²which He promised beforehand through His prophets in the holy Scriptures,

³concerning His Son, who was born of a descendant of David according to the flesh,

⁴who was declared the Son of God with power by the resurrection from the dead, according to the Spirit of holiness, Jesus Christ our Lord,

⁵through whom we have received grace and apostleship to bring about the obedience of faith among all the Gentiles for His name's sake,

⁶among whom you also are the called of Jesus Christ;

⁷to all who are beloved of God in Rome, called as saints: Grace to you and peace from God our Father and the Lord Jesus Christ.

⁸First, I thank my God through Jesus Christ for you all, because your faith is being proclaimed throughout the whole world.

⁹For God, whom I serve in my spirit in the preaching of the gospel of His Son, is my witness as to how unceasingly I make mention of you,

¹⁰always in my prayers making request, if perhaps now at last by the will of God I may succeed in coming to you.

¹¹For I long to see you so that I may impart some spiritual gift to you, that you may be established;

¹²that is, that I may be encouraged together with you while

among you, each of us by the other's faith, both yours and mine.

¹³I do not want you to be unaware, brethren, that often I have planned to come to you (and have been prevented so far) so that I may obtain some fruit among you also, even as among the rest of the Gentiles.

¹⁴I am under obligation both to Greeks and to barbarians, both to the wise and to the foolish.

¹⁵So, for my part, I am eager to preach the gospel to you also who are in Rome.

¹⁶For I am not ashamed of the gospel, for it is the power of God for salvation to everyone who believes, to the Jew first and also to the Greek.

¹⁷For in it the righteousness of God is revealed from faith to faith; as it is written, "BUT THE RIGHTEOUS man SHALL LIVE BY FAITH."

 QUESTIONS

1. Who wrote Romans?

_____

_____

_____

2. What does gospel mean?

_____

_____

_____

3. Where did the gospel originate?

_____

_____

_____

4. In Verse 3 and 4 who does Paul say Christ is?

a. _____

b. _____

5. What is Paul's ultimate reason for writing Romans?

_____

_____

_____

6. What is Paul's immediate reason for writing Romans, in Chapter one?

_____

_____

_____

7. Who was preventing Paul from getting to Rome?

_____

_____

_____

8. What are the two key verses in the book of Romans?

_____

_____

_____

9. In Habakkuk 2:4 who will live by his faith?

_____

_____

_____

Application QUESTIONS ●▶

1. God was preventing Paul from going to Rome because He wanted him out spreading the gospel and planting churches. Getting together with Christians was secondary. Is spreading the gospel a priority to you? Why or why not?

_____

_____

_____

2. It says in Chapter one, Verse 16, "It is the power of God for salvation for everyone who believes." Are you trusting in God for your salvation, or are you trusting in yourself and your works for salvation?

_____

_____

_____

3. Do you think our culture embraces Verse 16? Why or why not?

_____

_____

_____

4. How can you become more like Paul? He was a man who understood:

     a. Man's Nature? _____

     b. Condemnation?_____

     c. Hell? _____

     d. Salvation? _____

MEMORY VERSE

Romans 1:16-17
[16]For I am not ashamed of the gospel, for it is the power of God for salvation to everyone who believes, to the Jew first and also to the Greek. [17]For in it the righteousness of God is revealed from faith to faith; as it is written, " BUT THE RIGHTEOUS man SHALL LIVE BY FAITH."

PRAYER REQUESTS

_____

_____

_____

_____

_____

THE CONDEMNATION OF THE GENTILE
Romans 1:18-32

In session two Paul proves why man needs the righteousness of God. He tells of the self-evident truths that lead man to God. He speaks to the Gentile and why man is left with no excuse.

CHAPTER 1

¹⁸For the wrath of God is revealed from heaven against all ungodliness and unrighteousness of men who suppress the truth in unrighteousness,

¹⁹because that which is known about God is evident within them; for God made it evident to them.

²⁰For since the creation of the world His invisible attributes, His eternal power and divine nature, have been clearly seen, being understood through what has been made, so that they are without excuse.

²¹For even though they knew God, they did not honor Him as God or give thanks, but they became futile in their speculations, and their foolish heart was darkened.

²²Professing to be wise, they became fools,

²³and exchanged the glory of the incorruptible God for an image in the form of corruptible man and of birds and four-footed animals and crawling creatures.

²⁴Therefore God gave them over in the lusts of their hearts to impurity, so that their bodies would be dishonored among them.

²⁵For they exchanged the truth of God for a lie, and worshiped and served the creature rather than the Creator, who is blessed forever. Amen.

²⁶For this reason God gave them over to degrading passions; for their women exchanged the natural function for that which is unnatural,

²⁷and in the same way also the men abandoned the natural function of the woman and burned in their desire toward one another, men with men committing indecent acts and

receiving in their own persons the due penalty of their error.

²⁸And just as they did not see fit to acknowledge God any longer, God gave them over to a depraved mind, to do those things which are not proper,

²⁹being filled with all unrighteousness, wickedness, greed, evil; full of envy, murder, strife, deceit, malice; they are gossips,

³⁰slanderers, haters of God, insolent, arrogant, boastful, inventors of evil, disobedient to parents,

³¹without understanding, untrustworthy, unloving, unmerciful;

³²and although they know the ordinance of God, that those who practice such things are worthy of death, they not only do the same, but also give hearty approval to those who practice them.

 **QUESTIONS**

1. In 1:18 the wrath of God is revealed from heaven against all:

    a. _____

    b. _____

2. In 1:18 what do these men do?

_____

_____

_____

3. In 1:20 why is man without excuse?

_____

_____

_____

4. What does Rev. 21:8 say about the cowardly and unbelieving?

_____

_____

_____

5. In Verse 1:23 what did they exchange God for?

_____

_____

_____

6. What sin most depicts the wrath of God on a culture? Verses 26 and 27.

_____

_____

_____

UNPACKING *text*

Suppress - *katecho*
Wisdom - *filosofos, philosophers*

Application QUESTIONS ➤

1. Does the man in the Congo have a knowledge of God? How?

_____

_____

_____

2. How does man suppress the truth today in our culture?

_____

_____

_____

3. What does man replace God with today?

_____

_____

_____

4. How is our culture embracing the sin that most depicts the wrath of God (homosexuality)? What does this say about our culture?

_____

_____

_____

{ Homosexuality-"When man will do what animals instinctively will not."
"It is a scary place when there is no fear of God." }

5. Does man fear God today? Why or why not?

_____

_____

_____

6. Man is an inventor of evil. How is man inventing evil today?

_____

_____

_____

MEMORY VERSE

Romans 1:20
[20]For since the creation of the world His invisible attributes, His eternal power and divine nature, have been clearly seen, being understood through what has been made, so that they are without excuse.

PRAYER REQUESTS

_____

_____

_____

_____

_____

THE CONDEMNATION OF THE JEW:
LEGAL RIGHTEOUSNESS
Romans 2

In session three Paul sheds truth on the Jews and their way of thinking. Can the Jew earn the righteousness of God through works of the Law? He destroys the idea of legalism and tells them of true circumcision: circumcision of the heart.

CHAPTER 2

¹Therefore you have no excuse, everyone of you who passes judgment, for in that which you judge another, you condemn yourself; for you who judge practice the same things.

²And we know that the judgment of God rightly falls upon those who practice such things.

³But do you suppose this, O man, when you pass judgment on those who practice such things and do the same yourself, that you will escape the judgment of God?

⁴Or do you think lightly of the riches of His kindness and tolerance and patience, not knowing that the kindness of God leads you to repentance?

⁵But because of your stubbornness and unrepentant heart you are storing up wrath for yourself in the day of wrath and revelation of the righteous judgment of God,

⁶who WILL RENDER TO EACH PERSON ACCORDING TO HIS DEEDS:

⁷to those who by perseverance in doing good seek for glory and honor and immortality, eternal life;

⁸but to those who are selfishly ambitious and do not obey the truth, but obey unrighteousness, wrath and indignation.

⁹There will be tribulation and distress for every soul of man who does evil, of the Jew first and also of the Greek,

¹⁰but glory and honor and peace to everyone who does good, to the Jew first and also to the Greek.

¹¹For there is no partiality with God.

¹²For all who have sinned without the Law will also perish

without the Law, and all who have sinned under the Law will be judged by the Law;

¹³for it is not the hearers of the Law who are just before God, but the doers of the Law will be justified.

¹⁴For when Gentiles who do not have the Law do instinctively the things of the Law, these, not having the Law, are a law to themselves,

¹⁵in that they show the work of the Law written in their hearts, their conscience bearing witness and their thoughts alternately accusing or else defending them,

¹⁶on the day when, according to my gospel, God will judge the secrets of men through Christ Jesus.

¹⁷But if you bear the name "Jew" and rely upon the Law and boast in God,

¹⁸and know His will and approve the things that are essential, being instructed out of the Law,

¹⁹and are confident that you yourself are a guide to the blind, a light to those who are in darkness,

²⁰a corrector of the foolish, a teacher of the immature, having in the Law the embodiment of knowledge and of the truth,

²¹you, therefore, who teach another, do you not teach yourself? You who preach that one shall not steal, do you steal?

²²You who say that one should not commit adultery, do you commit adultery? You who abhor idols, do you rob temples?

²³You who boast in the Law, through your breaking the Law, do you dishonor God?

²⁴For "THE NAME OF GOD IS BLASPHEMED AMONG THE GENTILES BECAUSE OF YOU," just as it is written.

²⁵For indeed circumcision is of value if you practice the Law; but if you are a transgressor of the Law, your circumcision has become uncircumcision.

²⁶So if the uncircumcised man keeps the requirements of the Law, will not his uncircumcision be regarded as circumcision?

²⁷And he who is physically uncircumcised, if he keeps the Law, will he not judge you who though having the letter of the Law and circumcision are a transgressor of the Law?

²⁸For he is not a Jew who is one outwardly, nor is circumcision that which is outward in the flesh.

²⁹But he is a Jew who is one inwardly; and circumcision is that which is of the heart, by the Spirit, not by the letter; and his praise is not from men, but from God.

Text QUESTIONS

1. In Chapter 2:1, who is "you" referring to?

_____

_____

_____

2. In verse 4 where does Paul say God's kindness should lead?

_____

_____

_____

3. In verse 8, for "those who are selfishly ambitious," what awaits them?

_____

_____

_____

4. In verse 13 is there ever any man who could perfectly hear the Law and do the Law?

_____

_____

_____

5. What are the three ways, in verse 15, that the Gentile has the Law?
    1. _____
    2. _____
    3. _____

6. In verse 16, Who does God judge man through?

_____

_____

_____

7. In verse 29, what is true circumcision?

_____

_____

_____

UNPACKING *text*

> **Revelation** - *apokalypto*
> **Jew** - *the praise of God*

Application QUESTIONS ─────────➤

1. If you are going to try to earn your way to heaven, can you ever use the name Jesus?

_____

_____

_____

2. Is the Law of God on all men's conscience?

_____

_____

_____

3. Where do you seek your praise, from man or from God?

_____

_____

_____

MEMORY VERSE

Romans 2:29
²⁹But he is a Jew who is one inwardly; and circumcision is that which is of the heart, by the Spirit, not by the letter; and his praise is not from men, but from God.

ALL MEN ARE GUILTY

Romans 3:1-20

In session four Paul gives the estate that man is in, the extent of his sin, and the cause of it all. All men are guilty of sin. Not one man is righteous; he is dead, and he has no fear of God. In this session he also reveals why the Law exists.

CHAPTER 3

¹Then what advantage has the Jew? Or what is the benefit of circumcision?

²Great in every respect. First of all, that they were entrusted with the oracles of God.

³What then? If some did not believe, their unbelief will not nullify the faithfulness of God, will it?

⁴May it never be! Rather, let God be found true, though every man be found a liar, as it is written,
    "THAT YOU MAY BE JUSTIFIED IN YOUR WORDS, AND PREVAIL WHEN YOU ARE JUDGED."

⁵But if our unrighteousness demonstrates the righteousness of God, what shall we say? The God who inflicts wrath is not unrighteous, is He? (I am speaking in human terms.)

⁶May it never be! For otherwise, how will God judge the world?

⁷But if through my lie the truth of God abounded to His glory, why am I also still being judged as a sinner?

⁸And why not say (as we are slanderously reported and as some claim that we say), "Let us do evil that good may come"? Their condemnation is just.

⁹What then? Are we better than they? Not at all; for we have already charged that both Jews and Greeks are all under sin;

¹⁰as it is written, "THERE IS NONE RIGHTEOUS, NOT EVEN ONE;

¹¹THERE IS NONE WHO UNDERSTANDS, THERE IS NONE WHO SEEKS FOR GOD;

Man is under
sin

¹²ALL HAVE TURNED ASIDE, TOGETHER THEY HAVE BECOME USELESS; THERE IS NONE WHO DOES GOOD, THERE IS NOT EVEN ONE."

¹³THEIR THROAT IS AN OPEN GRAVE, WITH THEIR TONGUES THEY KEEP DECEIVING";
"THE POISON OF ASPS IS UNDER THEIR LIPS";

¹⁴"WHOSE MOUTH IS FULL OF CURSING AND BITTERNESS,"

¹⁵"THEIR FEET ARE SWIFT TO SHED BLOOD,

¹⁶DESTRUCTION AND MISERY ARE IN THEIR PATHS,

¹⁷AND THE PATH OF PEACE THEY HAVE NOT KNOWN."

¹⁸"THERE IS NO FEAR OF GOD BEFORE THEIR EYES."

¹⁹Now we know that whatever the Law says, it speaks to those who are under the Law, so that every mouth may be closed and all the world may become accountable to God;

²⁰because by the works of the Law no flesh will be justified in His sight; for through the Law comes the knowledge of sin.

man will drive a nail in that hand – man is an enemy of God

there is no excuse – everyone is accountable

to reveal your sin

Text QUESTIONS

1. In Verse 3 and 4, do the Jews get a free pass simply because they are Jews?

_____

_____

_____

2. In Verse 6 who is judged?

_____

_____

_____

3. In Verse 8 what does Paul say to those who say, "from evil comes good"?

_____

_____

_____

4. In Verse 9 the Jews are asking if they are better than the Gentiles. What does Scrip
say here?

_____

_____

_____

5. What is the estate of man in Verse 10?

_____

_____

_____

6. What is the extent of man's guilt in Verse 11?

_____

_____

_____

7. What is the effect of man in Verse 12?

_____

_____

_____

8. In Verse 20 what is the purpose of the Law?

_____

_____

_____

UNPACKING *text*

Dead - *in Greek is dead*

Application QUESTIONS

1. Does man fear God today?

_____
_____
_____

2. What does man think about hell/judgment?

_____
_____
_____

3. The Law was given to show us our sin. Does this drive you to your knees? Why or why not?

___Yes!_____
_____
_____

4. The expression of sin is how you treat people and how you speak to people. How are you doing?

_____
_____
We must be a new creation!
Sovereign act of grace upon dead

JUSTIFICATION:
SALVATION

Romans 3:21-31

In session five Paul tells the Jews and Gentiles how to be saved. He explains that there is no human help involved. It is apart from the Law. It is through faith in Jesus Christ alone.

CHAPTER 3

[21]But now apart from the Law the righteousness of God has been manifested, being witnessed by the Law and the Prophets,

[22]even the righteousness of God through faith in Jesus Christ for all those who believe; for there is no distinction;

[23]for all have sinned and fall short of the glory of God,

[24]being justified as a gift by His grace through the redemption which is in Christ Jesus;

[25]whom God displayed publicly as a propitiation in His blood through faith. This was to demonstrate His righteousness, because in the forbearance of God He passed over the sins previously committed;

[26]for the demonstration, I say, of His righteousness at the present time, so that He would be just and the justifier of the one who has faith in Jesus.

[27]Where then is boasting? It is excluded By what kind of law? Of works? No, but by a law of faith.

[28]For we maintain that a man is justified by faith apart from works of the Law.

[29]Or is God the God of Jews only? Is He not the God of Gentiles also? Yes, of Gentiles also,

[30]since indeed God who will justify the circumcised by faith and the uncircumcised through faith is one.

[31]Do we then nullify the Law through faith? May it never be! On the contrary, we establish the Law.

# Text QUESTIONS

1. In 3:22 the righteousness of God is revealed how and through Whom?

_____

_____

_____

2. For whom?

_____

_____

_____

3. What was the payment or the redemption of our sin? Verse 3:24.

_____

_____

_____

4. Why was Christ's death displayed publicly? Verse 3:25.

_____

_____

_____

5. Why could God forgive an Old Testament man? Verse 3:26.

_____

_____

_____

6. How, in 3:28, is a man justified? What is it apart from?

_____

_____

_____

7. Is the Law now worthless? What then is it? Verse 3:31.

_____

_____

_____

UNPACKING *text*

Manifest - *apocolypto, "apo" (the covers) "colupto" (back)*
Revelation - *the apocolyps, the pulling back of the covers*
Propitiation - *to satisfy wrath*

Application QUESTIONS ———————➤

1. When you pull back the covers of righteousness, what do you see? The command-ments/Law? Or the Cross? What should we see?

_____

_____

_____

{ "The righteousness of God is not earned by man. It is unveiled by God. It's a present." }

2. Christ died as a payment to the justice of God. God is not tame. God is Holy. How does this settle with our culture today?

_____

_____

_____

3. If God was a compromising God there would be no justice in Him. Why do people want this kind of God?

_____

_____

_____

4. What will you say if someone says to you, "How can a loving God send a man to hell?"

_____

_____

_____

MEMORY VERSE

Romans 3:23-24
[23]for all have sinned and fall short of the glory of God, [24]being justified as a gift by His grace through the redemption which is in Christ Jesus;

PRAYER REQUESTS

_____

_____

_____

_____

_____

HOW WE ARE NOT SAVED:
HOW WE ARE SAVED BY THE EXAMPLE OF ABRAHAM

Romans 4

In session six Paul gives an example of one saved by faith. Paul teaches that we aren't saved by Law, works, or religion. We are to follow the path of Abraham. He believed in the power of God and the promise of God. What then, 4000 years ago, was Abraham's hope in? Jesus Christ.

CHAPTER 4

¹What then shall we say that Abraham, our forefather according to the flesh, has found?

²For if Abraham was justified by works, he has something to boast about, but not before God.

³For what does the Scripture say? "ABRAHAM BELIEVED GOD, AND IT WAS CREDITED TO HIM AS RIGHTEOUSNESS."

⁴Now to the one who works, his wage is not credited as a favor, but as what is due.

⁵But to the one who does not work, but believes in Him who justifies the ungodly, his faith is credited as righteousness,

⁶just as David also speaks of the blessing on the man to whom God credits righteousness apart from works:

⁷"BLESSED ARE THOSE WHOSE LAWLESS DEEDS HAVE BEEN FORGIVEN, AND WHOSE SINS HAVE BEEN COVERED.

⁸"BLESSED IS THE MAN WHOSE SIN THE LORD WILL NOT TAKE INTO ACCOUNT."

⁹Is this blessing then on the circumcised, or on the uncircumcised also? For we say, "FAITH WAS CREDITED TO ABRAHAM AS RIGHTEOUSNESS."

¹⁰How then was it credited? While he was circumcised, or uncircumcised? Not while circumcised, but while uncircumcised;

¹¹and he received the sign of circumcision, a seal of the righteousness of the faith which he had while uncircumcised,

so that he might be the father of all who believe without being circumcised, that righteousness might be credited to them,

¹²and the father of circumcision to those who not only are of the circumcision, but who also follow in the steps of the faith of our father Abraham which he had while uncircumcised.

¹³For the promise to Abraham or to his descendants that he would be heir of the world was not through the Law, but through the righteousness of faith.

¹⁴For if those who are of the Law are heirs, faith is made void and the promise is nullified;

¹⁵for the Law brings about wrath, but where there is no law, there also is no violation.

¹⁶For this reason it is by faith, in order that it may be in accordance with grace, so that the promise will be guaranteed to all the descendants, not only to those who are of the Law, but also to those who are of the faith of Abraham, who is the father of us all,

¹⁷(as it is written, "A FATHER OF MANY NATIONS HAVE I MADE YOU") in the presence of Him whom he believed, even God, who gives life to the dead and calls into being that which does not exist.

¹⁸In hope against hope he believed, so that he might become a father of many nations according to that which had been spoken, "SO SHALL YOUR DESCENDANTS BE."

¹⁹Without becoming weak in faith he contemplated his own body, now as good as dead since he was about a hundred years old, and the deadness of Sarah's womb;

²⁰yet, with respect to the promise of God, he did not waver in unbelief but grew strong in faith, giving glory to God,

²¹and being fully assured that what God had promised, He was able also to perform.

²²Therefore IT WAS ALSO CREDITED TO HIM AS RIGHTEOUSNESS.

²³Now not for his sake only was it written that it was credited to him,

²⁴but for our sake also, to whom it will be credited, as those who believe in Him who raised Jesus our Lord from the dead,

²⁵He who was delivered over because of our transgressions, and was raised because of our justification.

Text QUESTIONS

1. In Verse 3 what did Abraham believe to have righteousness reckoned to him?

_____

_____

_____

2. Besides Abraham, who else is given as an example as an Old Testament Christian?

_____

_____

_____

3. How, in Verse 6, is David reckoned as righteous?

_____

_____

_____

4. In 4:10, was Abraham's faith reckoned to him as righteousness because he was circumcised?

_____

_____

_____

5. Circumcision was the sign/seal of a promise God made to Abraham. What was the promise? Verse 4:13.

_____

_____

_____

6. What does 4:16 say about "the promise"?

_____

_____

_____

7. What is 4:21 referring to?

_____

_____

_____

UNPACKING _text_

4:1 **found** - _eureka_

4:3 **reckoned** - _credited, imputed_

Application QUESTIONS ━━━━━━▸

1. Why is 4:3 a shock to the Jews?

_____

_____

_____

2. Abraham was reckoned righteous without circumcision (his faith was without works or religion). How is this difficult for the "religious" man today?

_____

_____

_____

3. What does it mean to have the faith of Abraham?

_____

_____

_____

4. Do you know how to share the gospel? How?

_____

_____

_____

PRAYER REQUESTS

_____

_____

_____

_____

_____

NOTES

SECURITY IN SALVATION

Romans 5:1-14

In session seven Paul teaches of the security we have in our salvation. We have security because of the past, the present, and the future. Our hope rests in Him, not in us. It is because of His love we know He will never lose us. Paul also teaches that if all men are assured of death through one man (Adam), then we can be assured of our life through Jesus Christ.

CHAPTER 5

¹Therefore, having been justified by faith, we have peace with God through our Lord Jesus Christ,

²through whom also we have obtained our introduction by faith into this grace in which we stand; and we exult in hope of the glory of God.

³And not only this, but we also exult in our tribulations, knowing that tribulation brings about perseverance;

⁴and perseverance, proven character; and proven character, hope;

⁵and hope does not disappoint, because the love of God has been poured out within our hearts through the Holy Spirit who was given to us.

⁶For while we were still helpless, at the right time Christ died for the ungodly.

⁷For one will hardly die for a righteous man; though perhaps for the good man someone would dare even to die.

⁸But God demonstrates His own love toward us, in that while we were yet sinners, Christ died for us.

⁹Much more then, having now been justified by His blood, we shall be saved from the wrath of God through Him.

¹⁰For if while we were enemies we were reconciled to God through the death of His Son, much more, having been reconciled, we shall be saved by His life.

¹¹ And not only this, but we also exult in God through our Lord Jesus Christ, through whom we have now received the reconciliation.

¹²Therefore, just as through one man sin entered into the world, and death through sin, and so death spread to all men, because all sinned-

¹³for until the Law sin was in the world, but sin is not imputed when there is no law.

¹⁴Nevertheless death reigned from Adam until Moses, even over those who had not sinned in the likeness of the offense of Adam, who is a type of Him who was to come.

Text QUESTIONS ———————————————►

1. In 5:1 what does "having been justified by faith" mean?

_____

_____

_____

2. What does trial bring? Verse 5:3.

_____

_____

_____

3. What does perseverance bring? Verse 5:4.

_____

_____

_____

4. What does character bring? Verse 5:4.

_____

_____

_____

5. In Verse 10 we were reconciled to God through what?

_____

_____

_____

6. In Verse 10 we are saved by what?

_____

_____

_____

7. Who is the "one man" through whom sin entered the world? Verse 5:12.

_____

_____

_____

8. Who does the death spread to? Verse 5:12.

_____

_____

_____

UNPACKING *text*

Proof - *dokimi*

Application QUESTIONS

1. How could you prove to someone that you are saved?

_____

_____

_____

2. Can you lose your salvation?

_____

_____

_____

3. God loved you before you were saved. Do you think He will love you any less after you are saved?

_____

_____

_____

4. Are you humble about what God did for you or do you rejoice in it?

_____

_____

_____

5. Why is it so radical for a culture to hear that we can have assurance of salvation through the activity of someone else?

_____

_____

_____

MEMORY VERSE

Romans 5:9
⁹Much more then, having now been justified by His blood, we shall be saved from the wrath of God through Him.

GRACE

Romans 5:15-21

In session eight Paul tells us how broad and how deep God's love is for us. Paul shows that sin no longer reigns in us, but grace. And because of His grace, we will reign with Him forevermore.

CHAPTER 5

[15]But the free gift is not like the transgression. For if by the transgression of the one the many died, much more did the grace of God and the gift by the grace of the one Man, Jesus Christ, abound to the many.

[16]The gift is not like that which came through the one who sinned; for on the one hand the judgment arose from one transgression resulting in condemnation, but on the other hand the free gift arose from many transgressions resulting in justification.

[17]For if by the transgression of the one, death reigned through the one, much more those who receive the abundance of grace and of the gift of righteousness will reign in life through the One, Jesus Christ.

[18]So then as through one transgression there resulted con-demnation to all men, even so through one act of righteous-ness there resulted justification of life to all men.

[19]For as through the one man's disobedience the many were made sinners, even so through the obedience of the One the many will be made righteous.

[20]The Law came in so that the transgression would increase; but where sin increased, grace abounded all the more,

[21]so that, as sin reigned in death, even so grace would reign through righteousness to eternal life through Jesus Christ our Lord.

Text QUESTIONS

1. In Romans 5:16 the judgment arose from how many transgressions? Resulting in what?

_____

_____

_____

2. The free gift arose from how many transgressions? Resulting in what?

_____

_____

_____

3. What was the one act of righteousness in verse 18?

_____

_____

_____

4. Jesus said, "Not My will but _____."

_____

_____

_____

5. Adam said, "Not Thy will but _____."

_____

_____

_____

6. When sin increased, what increased all the more?

_____

_____

_____

Gethsemane - *the olive crush*

Application QUESTIONS ━━━━━━━━━➤

1. Can we be certain that God can curse the sin of man? How?

_____

_____

_____

2. Can we be certain that God will bless us through His mercy? How?

_____

_____

_____

3. In what area of your life do you need to say, "Not my will, but Thy will"?

_____

_____

_____

{
"With Adam, man was lost at a tree. With Jesus, man was gained at a tree."

"One day the only way we will know Satan existed is by the wounds on Christ's hands."
}

4. Look again at Revelation 22:1-5. Who do you need to share the gospel with so that they too can reign with Him forever?

_____

_____

_____

MEMORY VERSE

Romans 5:20-21

[20]"The Law came in so that the transgression would increase; but where sin increased, grace abounded all the more, [21]so that, as sin reigned in death, even so grace would reign through righteousness to eternal life through Jesus Christ our Lord.

PRAYER REQUESTS

ANTINOMIANISM:
SANCTIFICATION

Romans 6:1-12

In session nine Paul teaches that we are saved from the penalty of sin, we are being saved from the power of sin, and we will be saved from the presence of sin. He shows us that we are a new creation in Jesus Christ.

CHAPTER 6

¹What shall we say then? Are we to continue in sin so that grace may increase?

²May it never be! How shall we who died to sin still live in it?

³Or do you not know that all of us who have been baptized into Christ Jesus have been baptized into His death?

⁴Therefore we have been buried with Him through baptism into death, so that as Christ was raised from the dead through the glory of the Father, so we too might walk in newness of life.

⁵For if we have become united with Him in the likeness of His death, certainly we shall also be in the likeness of His resurrection,

⁶knowing this, that our old self was crucified with Him, in order that our body of sin might be done away with, so that we would no longer be slaves to sin;

⁷for he who has died is freed from sin.

⁸Now if we have died with Christ, we believe that we shall also live with Him,

⁹knowing that Christ, having been raised from the dead, is never to die again; death no longer is master over Him.

¹⁰For the death that He died, He died to sin once for all; but the life that He lives, He lives to God.

¹¹Even so consider yourselves to be dead to sin, but alive to God in Christ Jesus.

¹²Therefore do not let sin reign in your mortal body so that you obey its lusts,

Text QUESTIONS

1. What is the immediate problem in 6:1?

_____

_____

_____

2. Does Christianity lead to sin? Verse 6:2.

_____

_____

_____

3. In Verse 3 what two actions have taken place?

_____

_____

_____

4. What has happened to us in Verse 4a?

_____

_____

_____

5. What action is taking place now in 4b?

_____

_____

_____

6. Verse 5 says, "If we have been _____ with Him, then _____, we shall be in the likeness of His resurrection." Do we only get one and not the other?

_____

_____

_____

7. What is the Christian creed?

_____

_____

_____

UNPACKING *text*

Sanctification - *set apart, to make holy*
United - *graphed in*
Mortal - *morti, death*

Application QUESTIONS ————————➤

1. Can you do whatever you want since you can't lose your salvation (antinomianism)?

_____

_____

_____

2. The issue with man is not whether we will be free. It is which master will we be under, Christ or Satan. Who is your master? Who is more destructive, and Who is more freeing?

_____

_____

_____

{ "We are not sinless, but we sin less." }

3. Since you were born again, how has your relationship to sin changed?

_____

_____

_____

4. What can you do to help with the struggle of sin?

_____

_____

_____

MEMORY VERSE

Romans 6:8-10
⁸Now if we have died with Christ, we believe that we shall also live with Him, ⁹knowing that Christ, having been raised from the dead, is never to die again; death no longer is master over Him. ¹⁰For the death that He died, He died to sin once for all; but the life that He lives, He lives to God.

PRAYER REQUESTS

_____

_____

_____

_____

_____

WE MUST OBEY:
THE GENTILE ILLUSTRATION
Romans 6:13-23

Is it better to have the rule outside of you or inside of you? In session ten we learn what it means to be obedient from the heart. As Christians, we have taken up residence in the body of Christ! His gift to you, His free gift to you, is eternal life!

CHAPTER 6

¹³and do not go on presenting the members of your body to sin as instruments of unrighteousness; but present yourselves to God as those alive from the dead, and your members as instruments of righteousness to God.

¹⁴For sin shall not be master over you, for you are not under law but under grace.

¹⁵What then? Shall we sin because we are not under law but under grace? May it never be!

¹⁶Do you not know that when you present yourselves to someone as slaves for obedience, you are slaves of the one whom you obey, either of sin resulting in death, or of obedience resulting in righteousness?

¹⁷But thanks be to God that though you were slaves of sin, you became obedient from the heart to that form of teaching to which you were committed,

¹⁸and having been freed from sin, you became slaves of righteousness.

¹⁹ I am speaking in human terms because of the weakness of your flesh For just as you presented your members as slaves to impurity and to lawlessness, resulting in further lawlessness, so now present your members as slaves to righteousness, resulting in sanctification.

²⁰For when you were slaves of sin, you were free in regard to righteousness.

²¹Therefore what benefit were you then deriving from the things of which you are now ashamed? For the outcome of those things is death.

²²But now having been freed from sin and enslaved to God, you derive your benefit, resulting in sanctification, and the outcome, eternal life.

²³For the wages of sin is death, but the free gift of God is eternal life in Christ Jesus our Lord.

Text QUESTIONS

1. As a sinner, what comfort do you find in 6:14?

_____

_____

_____

2. In 6:16 what is the result of being a slave to sin?

_____

_____

_____

3. What then is the result of being obedient?

_____

_____

_____

4. In Verse 19 what was the result of lawlessness?

_____

_____

_____

5. What was the result of righteousness?

_____

_____

_____

6. In 6:21 what is the outcome of "the things of which you are now ashamed"?

_____

_____

_____

7. In 6:22 what is the outcome of "being enslaved to God"?

_____

_____

_____

8. What is the wage of sin?

_____

_____

_____

9. What is the free gift of God?

_____

_____

_____

UNPACKING *text*

Wages - *the soldier's pay*

Application QUESTIONS

1. What does it mean to submit because you are under grace?

_____

_____

_____

2. As a Christian why do you now want to go to church, pray, confess, etc?

_____

_____

_____

{ "There is no such thing as a conversionless conversion." }

3. How does "there is no such thing as an unconverted Christian" challenge most people's ideas of Christianity today?

_____

_____

_____

MEMORY VERSE

Romans 6:23
²³For the wages of sin is death, but the free gift of God is eternal life in Christ Jesus our Lord.

PRAYER REQUESTS

_____

_____

_____

_____

_____

Eleven

WE MUST OBEY:
THE JEWISH ILLUSTRATION, THE TESTIMONY OF PAUL

Romans 7:1-8:4

As Christians we are no longer slaves to sin. We are a new creation. However, we will still struggle with sin until the day we are in heaven. Paul teaches us how to fight well. In this session, we learn that "there is no condemnation for those who are in Christ Jesus."

CHAPTER 7

¹Or do you not know, brethren (for I am speaking to those who know the law), that the law has jurisdiction over a person as long as he lives?

²For the married woman is bound by law to her husband while he is living; but if her husband dies, she is released from the law concerning the husband.

³So then, if while her husband is living she is joined to another man, she shall be called an adulteress; but if her husband dies, she is free from the law, so that she is not an adulteress though she is joined to another man.

⁴Therefore, my brethren, you also were made to die to the Law through the body of Christ, so that you might be joined to another, to Him who was raised from the dead, in order that we might bear fruit for God.

⁵For while we were in the flesh, the sinful passions, which were aroused by the Law, were at work in the members of our body to bear fruit for death.

⁶But now we have been released from the Law, having died to that by which we were bound, so that we serve in newness of the Spirit and not in oldness of the letter.

⁷What shall we say then? Is the Law sin? May it never be! On the contrary, I would not have come to know sin except through the Law; for I would not have known about coveting if the Law had not said, "YOU SHALL NOT COVET."

⁸But sin, taking opportunity through the commandment, produced in me coveting of every kind; for apart from the Law sin is dead.

⁹I was once alive apart from the Law; but when the commandment came, sin became alive and I died;

¹⁰and this commandment, which was to result in life, proved to result in death for me;

¹¹for sin, taking an opportunity through the commandment, deceived me and through it, killed me.

¹²So then, the Law is holy, and the commandment is holy and righteous and good.

¹³Therefore did that which is good become a cause of death for me? May it never be! Rather it was sin, in order that it might be shown to be sin by effecting my death through that which is good, so that through the commandment sin would become utterly sinful.

¹⁴For we know that the Law is spiritual, but I am of flesh, sold into bondage to sin.

¹⁵For what I am doing, I do not understand; for I am not practicing what I would like to do, but I am doing the very thing I hate.

¹⁶But if I do the very thing I do not want to do, I agree with the Law, confessing that the Law is good.

¹⁷So now, no longer am I the one doing it, but sin which dwells in me.

¹⁸For I know that nothing good dwells in me, that is, in my flesh; for the willing is present in me, but the doing of the good is not.

¹⁹For the good that I want, I do not do, but I practice the very evil that I do not want.

²⁰But if I am doing the very thing I do not want, I am no longer the one doing it, but sin which dwells in me.

²¹I find then the principle that evil is present in me, the one who wants to do good.

²²For I joyfully concur with the law of God in the inner man,

²³but I see a different law in the members of my body, waging war against the law of my mind and making me a prisoner of the law of sin which is in my members.

²⁴Wretched man that I am! Who will set me free from the body of this death?

²⁵Thanks be to God through Jesus Christ our Lord! So then, on the one hand I myself with my mind am serving the law of God, but on the other, with my flesh the law of sin.

CHAPTER 8

¹Therefore there is now no condemnation for those who are in Christ Jesus.

²For the law of the Spirit of life in Christ Jesus has set you free from the law of sin and of death.

³For what the Law could not do, weak as it was through the flesh, God did: sending His own Son in the likeness of sinful flesh and as an offering for sin, He condemned sin in the flesh,

⁴so that the requirement of the Law might be fulfilled in us, who do not walk according to the flesh but according to the Spirit.

Text QUESTIONS

1. Who is "you" referring to in 7:4?

_____

_____

_____

2. If the Law is the "old husband", Who is the "new husband"? Verse 7:4,

_____

_____

_____

3. Since we are released from the Law, how do we serve? Verse 7:6.

_____

_____

_____

4. The Jews ask, "Is the Law sin?" What does the Law do? Verse 7:7.

_____

_____

_____

5. In Verse 11, what two things did "sin" do?

1. _____

2. _____

6. Even though we are saved from the wrath of sin, does sin still indwell in us? Verse 7:17.

_____

_____

_____

7. Paul asks, "Who will set me free from the body of this death?" Who will?

_____

_____

_____

{ "Walking in the power of the Spirit is yielding to the Spirit of God." }

Application QUESTIONS ———————➤

1. Can you have Christianity without the Holy Spirit? Why or why not?

_____

_____

_____

2. Why do you put your trust in God?

_____

_____

_____

3. Why is it difficult for Christians to accept that even though we have a "new nature", we still struggle with our "old man"?

_____

_____

_____

4. What does it mean that we do not walk according to the flesh but according to the Spirit?

_____

_____

_____

MEMORY VERSE

Romans 8:1
¹Therefore there is now no condemnation for those who are in Christ Jesus.

PRAYER REQUESTS

THE POWER OF THE HOLY SPIRIT:
VICTORY IN JESUS

Romans 8:5-39

In session twelve we learn that with salvation comes the Holy Spirit. We are now children of God, adopted as sons. Paul shows us that we have the Holy Spirit to help us in the struggle. What a great encouragement it is to know that when God is for us, no one can oppose us!

CHAPTER 8

⁵For those who are according to the flesh set their minds on the things of the flesh, but those who are according to the Spirit, the things of the Spirit.

⁶For the mind set on the flesh is death, but the mind set on the Spirit is life and peace,

⁷because the mind set on the flesh is hostile toward God; for it does not subject itself to the law of God, for it is not even able to do so,

⁸and those who are in the flesh cannot please God.

⁹However, you are not in the flesh but in the Spirit, if indeed the Spirit of God dwells in you. But if anyone does not have the Spirit of Christ, he does not belong to Him.

¹⁰If Christ is in you, though the body is dead because of sin, yet the spirit is alive because of righteousness.

¹¹But if the Spirit of Him who raised Jesus from the dead dwells in you, He who raised Christ Jesus from the dead will also give life to your mortal bodies through His Spirit who dwells in you.

¹²So then, brethren, we are under obligation, not to the flesh, to live according to the flesh-

¹³for if you are living according to the flesh, you must die; but if by the Spirit you are putting to death the deeds of the body, you will live.

¹⁴For all who are being led by the Spirit of God, these are sons of God.

¹⁵For you have not received a spirit of slavery leading to fear

again, but you have received a spirit of adoption as sons by which we cry out, "Abba! Father!"

¹⁶The Spirit Himself testifies with our spirit that we are children of God,

¹⁷and if children, heirs also, heirs of God and fellow heirs with Christ, if indeed we suffer with Him so that we may also be glorified with Him.

¹⁸For I consider that the sufferings of this present time are not worthy to be compared with the glory that is to be revealed to us.

¹⁹For the anxious longing of the creation waits eagerly for the revealing of the sons of God.

²⁰For the creation was subjected to futility, not willingly, but because of Him who subjected it, in hope

²¹that the creation itself also will be set free from its slavery to corruption into the freedom of the glory of the children of God.

²²For we know that the whole creation groans and suffers the pains of childbirth together until now.

²³And not only this, but also we ourselves, having the first fruits of the Spirit, even we ourselves groan within ourselves, waiting eagerly for our adoption as sons, the redemption of our body.

²⁴For in hope we have been saved, but hope that is seen is not hope; for who hopes for what he already sees?

²⁵But if we hope for what we do not see, with perseverance we wait eagerly for it.

²⁶In the same way the Spirit also helps our weakness; for we do not know how to pray as we should, but the Spirit Himself intercedes for us with groanings too deep for words;

²⁷and He who searches the hearts knows what the mind of the Spirit is, because He intercedes for the saints according to the will of God.

²⁸And we know that God causes all things to work together for good to those who love God, to those who are called according to His purpose.

²⁹For those whom He foreknew, He also predestined to become conformed to the image of His Son, so that He would be the firstborn among many brethren;

³⁰and these whom He predestined, He also called; and these whom He called, He also justified; and these whom He justified, He also glorified.

³¹What then shall we say to these things? If God is for us, who is against us?

³²He who did not spare His own Son, but delivered Him over for us all, how will He not also with Him freely give us all things?

³³Who will bring a charge against God's elect? God is the one who justifies.

³⁴Who is the one who condemns? Christ Jesus is He who died, yes, rather who was raised, who is at the right hand of God, who also intercedes for us.

³⁵Who will separate us from the love of Christ? Will tribulation, or distress, or persecution, or famine, or nakedness, or peril, or sword?

³⁶Just as it is written,
"FOR YOUR SAKE WE ARE BEING PUT TO DEATH ALL DAY LONG;
WE WERE CONSIDERED AS SHEEP TO BE SLAUGHTERED."

³⁷But in all these things we overwhelmingly conquer through Him who loved us.

³⁸For I am convinced that neither death, nor life, nor angels, nor principalities, nor things present, nor things to come, nor powers,

³⁹nor height, nor depth, nor any other created thing, will be able to separate us from the love of God, which is in Christ Jesus our Lord.

 QUESTIONS

1. In 8:6 the mind set on the flesh is what?

_____

_____

_____

2. In 8:9, if you are not in the flesh, Who lives in you?

_____

_____

_____

3. In 8:13, if you are living according to the flesh, what must happen?

_____

_____

_____

4. In 8:15 we have received a "spirit of adoption". In 8:17 we are also called what?

_____

_____

_____

5. In 8:26 the Spirit of God does what?

_____

_____

_____

6. In 8:37 how do we conquer?

_____

_____

_____

UNPACKING *text*

Under Obligation - *debtors*
Abba Father - *Abba, what the Jew would call God*
Father - *what the Greek would call God*
Predestined - *proorizo, the boundary is marked out*

Application QUESTIONS

1. Can you have Christianity without the Holy Spirit? Why or why not?

_____

_____

_____

2. Why do you put your trust in God?

_____

_____

_____

3. What are ways the Spirit helps you?

_____

_____

_____

4. If God sent His Son to die upon a cross, do you think He will forget about you?

_____

_____

_____

5. In 8:3 no one can separate us from the love of Christ. We will, however, experience tribulation. How does this differ with what many believe today?

_____

_____

_____

MEMORY VERSE

Romans 8:13b
13b but if by the Spirit you are putting to death the deeds of the body, you will live.

PRAYER REQUESTS

_____

_____

_____

_____

_____

NOTES

Appendix

ANSWERS TO THE QUESTIONS

Appendix

TEXT ANSWERS SESSION ONE:

1) Paul
2) good message
3) The Old Testament
4)   a) descendant of David
          b) Son of God
5) To bring us faith in Jesus Christ
6) Because he couldn't get to Rome
7) God
8) Romans 1:16-17
9) the righteous man

TEXT ANSWERS SESSION TWO:

1)   a) ungodliness
          b) unrighteousness
2) suppress the truth
3) Because man has known of God since the time of creation
4) They will be in the lake of fire
5) An image in the form of corruptible man or other creatures
6) homosexuality

TEXT ANSWERS SESSION THREE:

1) the Jew
2) repentance
3) wrath and indignation
4) no
5)   1) heart
          2) conscience
          3) thoughts
6) Jesus Christ
7) a change of heart produced by God's Spirit

TEXT ANSWERS SESSION FOUR:

1) no
2) the world
3) Their condemnation is just
4) not at all
5) none righteous
6) none who understands, none who seeks
7) have become useless
8) To show sin

TEXT ANSWERS SESSION FIVE:

1) faith in Jesus Christ
2) all who believe
3) Christ Jesus
4) To demonstrate His righteousness
5) his faith in Jesus
6) faith apart from works
7) No, established

TEXT ANSWERS SESSION SIX:

1) He believed God
2) David
3) apart from works
4) no
5) he would be heir of the world, through the righteousness of faith
6) it is certain
7) the sacrifice of Issac

TEXT ANSWERS SESSION SEVEN:

1) having been saved
2) perseverance
3) character
4) hope
5) the death of His Son
6) His life
7) Adam
8) all

TEXT ANSWERS SESSION EIGHT:

1) One, condemnation
2) Many, justification
3) Death on a cross
4) Thine
5) mine
6) grace

TEXT ANSWERS SESSION NINE:

1) Can I do whatever I want, since I can't lose my salvation?
2) no
3)   1) baptized into Christ Jesus
        2) baptized into His death
4) we have been buried with Him
5) we walk in newness of life
6) united, certainly
7) 6:8-10

TEXT ANSWERS SESSION TEN:

1) under grace
2) death
3) righteousness
4) further lawlessness
5) sanctification
6) death
7) eternal life
8) death
9) eternal life in Christ Jesus our Lord

TEXT ANSWERS SESSION ELEVEN:

1) the Jew
2) Jesus
3) in newness of the Spirit
4) No, it shows us our sin
5) deceived, killed
6) yes
7) God, through Jesus Christ

TEXT ANSWERS SESSION TWELVE:

1) death
2) the Spirit of God
3) you must die
4) heirs
5) helps our weakness, intercedes for us
6) through Him, who loved us

ANNOTATED NOTES FROM TOMMY NELSON

I. The Introduction 1:1-7

1 The author

4 The proof

5 The purpose

6 The scope

2. The source of the gospel

3 The focus

7 The recipients

Romans 1

¹Paul, a bond-servant of Christ Jesus, called as an apostle, set apart for the gospel of God,
²which He promised beforehand through His prophets in the holy Scriptures,
³concerning His Son, who was born of a descendant of David according to the flesh,
⁴who was declared the Son of God with power by the resurrection from the dead, according to the Spirit of holiness, Jesus Christ our Lord,
⁵through whom we have received grace and apostleship to bring about the obedience of faith among all the Gentiles for His name's sake,
⁶among whom you also are the called of Jesus Christ;
⁷to all who are beloved of God in Rome, called as saints: Grace to you and peace from God our Father and the Lord Jesus Christ.

II.

Paul's primary purpose in writing (8-15)
Why he had not come to Rome.
he shows 7 terms of longing

15:20-22
God had other plans

⁸First, I thank my God through Jesus Christ for you all, because your faith is being proclaimed throughout the whole world.
⁹For God, whom I serve in my spirit in the preaching of the gospel of His Son, is my witness as to how unceasingly I make mention of you,
¹⁰always in my prayers making request, if perhaps now at last by the will of God I may succeed in coming to you.
¹¹For I long to see you so that I may impart some spiritual gift to you, that you may be established;
¹²that is, that I may be encouraged together with you while among you, each of us by the other's faith, both yours and mine.
¹³I do not want you to be unaware, brethren, that often I have planned to come to you (and have been prevented so far) so that I may obtain some fruit among you also, even as among the rest of the Gentiles.
¹⁴I am under obligation both to Greeks and to barbarians, both to the wise and to the foolish.
¹⁵So, for my part, I am eager to preach the gospel to you also who are in Rome.

"fruit" i.e. a harvest of souls

The Theme of Romans 1:16-17

"Righteousness": "That which the Righteousness of God requires Him to Require"
It is not earned but "unveiled" before man by an act of God.

¹⁶For I am not ashamed of the gospel, for it is the power of God for salvation to everyone who believes, to the Jew first and also to the Greek.
¹⁷For in it the righteousness of God is revealed from faith to faith; as it is written, "BUT THE RIGHTEOUS man SHALL LIVE BY FAITH."

Paul is not ashamed of the gospel because God saves through it

because the gospel alone provides Divine Righteousness.
– "faith to faith" –
from beginning to end Righteousness is procured by faith
– "faith alone" –

III.
The Need of Righteousness:
The Doctrine of Condemnation. First, the Condemnation of the Gentile
(1:18 – 3:20)   (1:18-32)
"is revealed": God's judgments in history upon idolatrous nations.

God's wrath is upon the Gentile world and their idolatry. (1:18-32)

¹⁸For the wrath of God is revealed from heaven against all ungodliness and unrighteousness of men who suppress the truth in unrighteousness,

he explains "suppressing truth"
He sees the knowledge of God in the creation...

..but will not bow..

homosexuality is highlighted as that sin that most depicts divine judgment

lit. "to retain God in their thinking"

lit. "a failed mind".

man rebels against common sense

and in a topsy-turvy world will elevate evil

salvation comes not through just knowing the truth

it. "according to truth"

.. No man will evade judgment by his heritage

19because that which is known about God is evident within them; for God made it evident to them.
20For since the creation of the world His invisible attributes, His eternal power and divine nature, have been clearly seen, being understood through what has been made, so that they are without excuse.
21For even though they knew God, they did not honor Him as God or give thanks, but they became futile in their speculations, and their foolish heart was darkened.
22Professing to be wise, they became fools,
23and exchanged the glory of the incorruptible God for an image in the form of corruptible man and of birds and four-footed animals and crawling creatures.
24Therefore God gave them over in the lusts of their hearts to impurity, so that their bodies would be dishonored among them.
25For they exchanged the truth of God for a lie, and worshiped and served the creature rather than the Creator, who is blessed forever. Amen.
26For this reason God gave them over to degrading passions; for their women exchanged the natural function for that which is unnatural,
27and in the same way also the men abandoned the natural function of the woman and burned in their desire toward one another, men with men committing indecent acts and receiving in their own persons the due penalty of their error.
28And just as they did not see fit to acknowledge God any longer, God gave them over to a depraved mind, to do those things which are not proper,
29being filled with all unrighteousness, wickedness, greed, evil; full of envy, murder, strife, deceit, malice; they are gossips,
30slanderers, haters of God, insolent, arrogant, boastful, inventors of evil, disobedient to parents,
31without understanding, untrustworthy, unloving, unmerciful;
32and although they know the ordinance of God, that those who practice such things are worthy of death, they not only do the same, but also give hearty approval to those who practice them.

B.
The Condemnation of the Jew
(ch. 2)

Romans 2
1Therefore you have no excuse, everyone of you who passes judgment, for in that which you judge another, you condemn yourself; for you who judge practice the same things.
2And we know that the judgment of God rightly falls upon those who practice such things.
3But do you suppose this, O man, when you pass judgment on those who practice such things and do the same yourself, that you will escape the judgment of God?
4Or do you think lightly of the riches of His kindness and tolerance and patience, not knowing that the kindness of God leads you to repentance?

Revelation

Rejection
Reasoning

Replacement

Reprobation

Ruin

Paul questions this absurd logic
i.e
"because He hasn't judged me He won't judge me."

⁵But because of your stubbornness and unrepentant heart you are storing up wrath for yourself in the day of wrath and revelation of the righteous judgment of God.

⁶who WILL RENDER TO EACH PERSON ACCORDING TO HIS DEEDS:

⁷to those who by perseverance in doing good seek for glory and honor and immortality, eternal life; *"contentious"*

⁸but to those who are selfishly ambitious and do not obey the truth, but obey unrighteousness, wrath and indignation.

⁹There will be tribulation and distress for every soul of man who does evil, of the Jew first and also of the Greek,

¹⁰but glory and honor and peace to everyone who does good, to the Jew first and also to the Greek.

¹¹For there is no partiality with God.

¹²For all who have sinned without the Law will also perish without the Law, and all who have sinned under the Law will be judged by the Law;

¹³for it is not the hearers of the Law who are just before God, but the doers of the Law will be justified.

¹⁴For when Gentiles who do not have the Law do instinctively the things of the Law, these, not having the Law, are a law to themselves,

¹⁵in that they show the work of the Law written in their hearts, their conscience bearing witness and their thoughts alternately accusing or else defending them,

¹⁶on the day when, according to my gospel, God will judge the secrets of men through Christ Jesus.

¹⁷But if you bear the name "Jew" and rely upon the Law and boast in God,

¹⁸and know His will and approve the things that are essential, being instructed out of the Law,

¹⁹and are confident that you yourself are a guide to the blind, a light to those who are in darkness,

²⁰a corrector of the foolish, a teacher of the immature, having in the Law the embodiment of knowledge and of the truth,

²¹you, therefore, who teach another, do you not teach yourself? You who preach that one shall not steal, do you steal?

²²You who say that one should not commit adultery, do you commit adultery? You who abhor idols, do you rob temples?

²³You who boast in the Law, through your breaking the Law, do you dishonor God?

²⁴For "THE NAME OF GOD IS BLASPHEMED AMONG THE GENTILES BECAUSE OF YOU," just as it is written.

²⁵For indeed circumcision is of value if you practice the Law; but if you are a transgressor of the Law, your circumcision has become uncircumcision.

²⁶So if the uncircumcised man keeps the requirements of the Law, will not his uncircumcision be regarded as circumcision?

²⁷And he who is physically uncircumcised, if he keeps the Law, will he not judge you who though having the letter of the Law and circumcision are a transgressor of the Law?

Handwritten margin notes (left):

the only time Jesus is mentioned in this section is as judge

But in contrast to the Gentiles who had only a law of conscience, the Jew had the revealed law of God.

Handwritten margin notes (right):

There is an appointed day of judgment when all sin will come due ... and deeds judged

Here is what a true "legal righteousness" would look like

— and here is the promise of judgment for sin

all who sin will be judged

all who obey perfectly will be saved

all sinners, Jew and Gentile, will be judged ...

.. all the obedient saved

Can Gentiles know the law? Yes.

they are to know.. ..to do..

..and to bless the nations

But ... 5 penetrating questions

instead of being a blessing they were a blasphemy

Circumcision can save only if you do the law

So if circumcision and law do not save, what is the advantage of being Jewish?

David's pronouncement that God is free to judge him after his adultery and murder

Here is Paul's doctrine of "total depravity"

Man's estate: Guilty

Sin's effect: dead to God

Sin's extent: mind
emotion
will

Sin's expression: wicked actions

²⁸For he is not a Jew who is one outwardly, nor is circumcision that which is outward in the flesh.
²⁹But he is a Jew who is one inwardly; and circumcision is that which is of the heart, by the Spirit, not by the letter: and his praise is not from men, but from God.

Romans 3
¹Then what advantage has the Jew? Or what is the benefit of circumcision?
²Great in every respect. First of all, that they were entrusted with the oracles of God.
³What then? If some did not believe, their unbelief will not nullify the faithfulness of God, will it?
⁴May it never be! Rather, let God be found true, though every man be found a liar, as it is written,
"THAT YOU MAY BE JUSTIFIED IN YOUR WORDS,
AND PREVAIL WHEN YOU ARE JUDGED."
⁵But if our unrighteousness demonstrates the righteousness of God, what shall we say? The God who inflicts wrath is not unrighteous, is He? (I am speaking in human terms.)
⁶May it never be! For otherwise, how will God judge the world?
⁷But if through my lie the truth of God abounded to His glory, why am I also still being judged as a sinner?
⁸And why not say (as we are slanderously reported and as some claim that we say), "Let us do evil that good may come"? Their condemnation is just.

C. The Condemnation of all men
(3:9-20)

⁹What then? Are we better than they? Not at all; for we have already charged that both Jews and Greeks are all under sin;
¹⁰as it is written,
"THERE IS NONE RIGHTEOUS, NOT EVEN ONE;
¹¹THERE IS NONE WHO UNDERSTANDS,
THERE IS NONE WHO SEEKS FOR GOD;
¹²ALL HAVE TURNED ASIDE, TOGETHER THEY HAVE BECOME USELESS;
THERE IS NONE WHO DOES GOOD, THERE IS NOT EVEN ONE."
¹³"THEIR THROAT IS AN OPEN GRAVE, WITH THEIR TONGUES THEY KEEP DECEIVING,"
"THE POISON OF ASPS IS UNDER THEIR LIPS";
¹⁴WHOSE MOUTH IS FULL OF CURSING AND BITTERNESS";
¹⁵"THEIR FEET ARE SWIFT TO SHED BLOOD,
¹⁶DESTRUCTION AND MISERY ARE IN THEIR PATHS,

They possessed the very word of God

Does God's judgment of the Jew make Him false?

No, God is free to judge all mankind

Is it right for God to be glorified in my judgment?

If He can't judge the Jew then He can't judge the world

Paul plays the devil's advocate and follows the argument to its end..

..which is self-condemning

Conclusion. Is the Jew more righteous than the Gentile?

Paul introduces a new term..

man is "under the law" or subject to its penalties

all mouths are silent
all are accountable
all are disobedient to law

A. Paul's Assertion (21-31)

Paul's first Reference to Christ as Savior

" to declare as righteous "
" to buy a slave his freedom "
" to satisfy the wrath of a deity "

God had allowed sinners to continue in previous days

.. and in the present He is just in justifying sinners

B. Paul's Example of Saving Faith - Abraham

1. Abraham was not saved by good works but by faith

" to impute or place to the account of "

---

[17]AND THE PATH OF PEACE THEY HAVE NOT KNOWN."
[18]"THERE IS NO FEAR OF GOD BEFORE THEIR EYES."
[19]Now we know that whatever the Law says, it speaks to those who are under the Law. so that every mouth may be closed and all the world may become accountable to God;
[20]because by the works of the Law no flesh will be justified in His sight; for through the Law comes the knowledge of sin.

IV. Justification: The Provision of Righteousness (3:21 - 8:39)

[21]But now apart from the Law the righteousness of God has been manifested, being witnessed by the Law and the Prophets,
[22]even the righteousness of God through faith in Jesus Christ for all those who believe; for there is no distinction;
[23]for all have sinned and fall short of the glory of God,
[24]being justified as a gift by His grace through the redemption which is in Christ Jesus;
[25]whom God displayed publicly as a propitiation in His blood through faith This was to demonstrate His righteousness, because in the forbearance of God He passed over the sins previously committed;
[26]for the demonstration, I say, of His righteousness at the present time, so that He would be just and the justifier of the one who has faith in Jesus.
[27]Where then is boasting? It is excluded By what kind of law? Of works? No, but by a law of faith.
[28]For we maintain that a man is justified by faith apart from works of the Law.
[29]Or is God the God of Jews only? Is He not the God of Gentiles also? Yes, of Gentiles also,
[30]since indeed God who will justify the circumcised by faith and the uncircumcised through faith is one.
[31]Do we then nullify the Law through faith? May it never be! On the contrary, we establish the Law.

Romans 4
[1]What then shall we say that Abraham, our forefather according to the flesh, has found?
[2]For if Abraham was justified by works, he has something to boast about, but not before God.
[3]For what does the Scripture say? "ABRAHAM BELIEVED GOD, AND IT WAS CREDITED TO HIM AS RIGHTEOUSNESS."
[4]Now to the one who works, his wage is not credited as a favor, but as what is due.

[5]But to the one who does not work, but believes in Him who justifies the ungodly, his faith is credited as righteousness,
[6]just as David also speaks of the blessing on the man to whom God credits righteousness apart from works:

Paul drops a theological bomb The purpose of the law is not to save but to condemn.

Three Results:
· Boasting is excluded

· Sovereignty is extended

· law is established
   its purpose
      preaching   .. is Christ
      pattern
      penalty

---

⁷"BLESSED ARE THOSE WHOSE LAWLESS DEEDS HAVE BEEN FORGIVEN,
AND WHOSE SINS HAVE BEEN COVERED.
⁸"BLESSED IS THE MAN WHOSE SIN THE LORD WILL NOT TAKE INTO ACCOUNT."

---

2. Abraham was not saved by circumcision

Circumcision is only a "sign" of inward faith

and a "seal" or "certainty" that righteousness would be provided by the seed of Abraham — Jesus

Thus a true child of Abraham is a child of faith... not circumcision

⁹Is this blessing then on the circumcised, or on the uncircumcised also? For we say, "FAITH WAS CREDITED TO ABRAHAM AS RIGHTEOUSNESS."
¹⁰How then was it credited? While he was circumcised, or uncircumcised? Not while circumcised, but while uncircumcised;
¹¹and he received the sign of circumcision, a seal of the righteousness of the faith which he had while uncircumcised, so that he might be the father of all who believe without being circumcised, that righteousness might be credited to them,
¹²and the father of circumcision to those who not only are of the circumcision, but who also follow in the steps of the faith of our father Abraham which he had while uncircumcised.

---

3. Abraham was not saved by law

If obedience to law grants the Kingdom...
1 faith is nullified, and
2. the Kingdom is lost...
all the law brings is wrath.

¹³For the promise to Abraham or to his descendants that he would be heir of the world was not through the Law, but through the righteousness of faith.
¹⁴For if those who are of the Law are heirs, faith is made void and the promise is nullified;
¹⁵for the Law brings about wrath, but where there is no law, there also is no violation.

Israel's rule in the Kingdom of Christ will come through faith in Christ not the nation's obedience to law

---

4.

Here is the salvation of Abraham
- Grace through faith -

Scripture says Abraham will be a father to the Gentile also

His faith was in a God of the impossible as his body as well as Sarah's was "dead"

His faith was in the promise of God

His salvation was imputed as a gift

¹⁶For this reason it is by faith, in order that it may be in accordance with grace, so that the promise will be guaranteed to all the descendants, not only to those who are of the Law, but also to those who are of the faith of Abraham, who is the father of us all,
¹⁷(as it is written, "A FATHER OF MANY NATIONS HAVE I MADE YOU") in the presence of Him whom he believed, even God, who gives life to the dead and calls into being that which does not exist.
¹⁸In hope against hope he believed, so that he might become a father of many nations according to that which had been spoken, "SO SHALL YOUR DESCENDANTS BE."
¹⁹Without becoming weak in faith he contemplated his own body, now as good as dead since he was about a hundred years old, and the deadness of Sarah's womb;
²⁰yet, with respect to the promise of God, he did not waver in unbelief but grew strong in faith, giving glory to God,
²¹and being fully assured that what God had promised, He was able also to perform.
²²Therefore IT WAS ALSO CREDITED TO HIM AS RIGHTEOUSNESS.

Because of faith we have:
- peace with God
- a stance in grace
- hope of Glory

trials are not inconsistent with our salvation - Rather they are essential, they prove and assure

Our hope will not fail because God loves us... a love we experience in the Rebirth

The security of God's love
He loved us when we hated Him

Men do not love like this. Only God does

And if He loved us this much while sinners how much more as Sons

If Christ's death assures me of God's love - which occurred when I was lost...
.. how "much more" does His life assure me - now that I am saved, and He intercedes for me

Can one man's action indeed be credited to all "in Him"? Indeed it can - the example? Adam

He defends this idea of imputed sin

---

²³Now not for his sake only was it written that it was credited to him,
²⁴but for our sake also, to whom it will be credited, as those who believe in Him who raised Jesus our Lord from the dead.
²⁵He who was delivered over because of our transgressions, and was raised because of our justification.

V. The Security of Righteousness (ch. 5 and 8)

Romans 5
¹Therefore, having been justified by faith, we have peace with God through our Lord Jesus Christ,
²through whom also we have obtained our introduction by faith into this grace in which we stand; and we exult in hope of the glory of God.
³And not only this, but we also exult in our tribulations, knowing that tribulation brings about perseverance;
⁴and perseverance, proven character; and proven character, hope;
⁵and hope does not disappoint, because the love of God has been poured out within our hearts through the Holy Spirit who was given to us.

The first mention

⁶For while we were still helpless, at the right time Christ died for the ungodly.
⁷For one will hardly die for a righteous man; though perhaps for the good man someone would dare even to die.
⁸But God demonstrates His own love toward us, in that while we were yet sinners, Christ died for us.
⁹Much more then, having now been justified by His blood, we shall be saved from the wrath of God through Him.
¹⁰For if while we were enemies we were reconciled to God through the death of His Son, much more, having been reconciled, we shall be saved by His life.
¹¹And not only this, but we also exult in God through our Lord Jesus Christ, through whom we have now received the reconciliation.

¹²Therefore, just as through one man sin entered into the world, and death through sin, and so death spread to all men because all sinned—
¹³for until the Law sin was in the world, but sin is not imputed when there is no law.

And Abraham is the fatherly example to all

- We believe God gave life from the dead

- And we rest in the work and promise of another

"Reconciled": to be restored to pe[ace]

reconciled
- provisionally
- actually

The result? I can exult in heaven now as though I were already there

All "sinned" in Adam's federal action

There should be no death before law

But Christ's gift is even more .. certain..	[14]Nevertheless death reigned from Adam until Moses, even over those who had not sinned in the likeness of the offense of Adam, who is a type of Him who was to come. [15]But the free gift is not like the transgression. For if by the transgression of the one the many died, much more did the grace of God and the gift by the grace of the one Man, Jesus Christ, abound to the many.	But death conquered one out of one ..because of Adam's sin This imputation by Adam is a "type" of Christ
His gift is ... Broader... His gift raises higher 's Conclusion: "one ... to all.." He defines "justification of life" en are "made righteous" ul's assertion of Grace: The law produced sin and sin reigned through death But Grace has dethroned death through the righteousness of Jesus Christ.	[16]The gift is not like that which came through the one who sinned; for on the one hand the judgment arose from one transgression resulting in condemnation, but on the other hand the free gift arose from many transgressions resulting in justification. [17]For if by the transgression of the one, death reigned through the one, much more those who receive the abundance of grace and of the gift of righteousness will reign in life through the One, Jesus Christ. [18]So then as through one transgression there resulted condemnation to all men, even so through one act of righteousness there resulted justification of life to all men. [19]For as through the one man's disobedience the many were made sinners, even so through the obedience of the One the many will be made righteous. [20]The Law came in so that the transgression would increase; but where sin increased, grace abounded all the more, [21]so that, as sin reigned in death, even so grace would reign through righteousness to eternal life through Jesus Christ our Lord.	
e Antinomian Question	VI The Problem With Imputed Righteousness - Antinomianism (ch. 6-7)	
a question: ① a fact: We are "dead to sin". ② a constitutional change has occured. Lit. "engrafted" We share a life ⑤ -14 is the application. Four points.. ..First there is an axiom vv 8-10 Our source of life shall never end	**Romans 6** [1]What shall we say then? Are we to continue in sin so that grace may increase? [2]May it never be! How shall we who died to sin still live in it? [3]Or do you not know that all of us who have been baptized into Christ Jesus have been baptized into His death? [4]Therefore we have been buried with Him through baptism into death, so that as Christ was raised from the dead through the glory of the Father, so we too might walk in newness of life. [5]For if we have become united with Him in the likeness of His death, certainly we shall also be in the likeness of His resurrection, [6]knowing this, that our old self was crucified with Him, in order that our body of sin might be done away with, so that we would no longer be slaves to sin; [7]for he who has died is freed from sin. [8]Now if we have died with Christ, we believe that we shall also live with Him,	③ The means: vv3-5 we are "in Christ" What's true of Him is true of us. He died to the penalty and power of sin - So did we. He rose in newness - so do we and this is a "certainty" ④ An explanation: vv 6-7 our old self was crucified abolished.. ..and we are free

9knowing that Christ, having been raised from the dead, is never to die again; death no longer is master over Him.
10For the death that He died, He died to sin once for all; but the life that He lives, He lives to God.

- "Next.. an attitude follows. (v 11)
We see ourselves differently
- Then there are actions:
  - we resist sin's reign
  - we present ourselves to God

11Even so consider yourselves to be dead to sin, but alive to God in Christ Jesus.
12Therefore do not let sin reign in your mortal body so that you obey its lusts,
13and do not go on presenting the members of your body to sin as instruments of unrighteousness; but present yourselves to God as those alive from the dead, and your members as instruments of righteousness to God.
14For sin shall not be master over you, for you are not under law but under grace.

- And there is an assurance (v14)
Sin will not master us
because we have a new master -
we are "under Grace"

Another question is raised: —
"would we ever take advantage of grace?"
The answer? "No. We must obey our new master - grace."

15What then? Shall we sin because we are not under law but under grace? May it never be!
16Do you not know that when you present yourselves to someone as slaves for obedience, you are slaves of the one whom you obey, either of sin resulting in death, or of obedience resulting in righteousness?
17But thanks be to God that though you were slaves of sin, you became obedient from the heart to that form of teaching to which you were committed, > i.e. entrusted
18and having been freed from sin, you became slaves of righteousness.
19I am speaking in human terms because of the weakness of your flesh For just as you presented your members as slaves to impurity and to lawlessness, resulting in further lawlessness, so now present your members as slaves to righteousness, resulting in sanctification.
20For when you were slaves of sin, you were free in regard to righteousness.
21Therefore what benefit were you then deriving from the things of which you are now ashamed? For the outcome of those things is death.
22But now having been freed from sin and enslaved to God, you derive your benefit, resulting in sanctification, and the outcome, eternal life.
23For the wages of sin is death, but the free gift of God is eternal life in Christ Jesus our Lord.

Paul supports the idea of being "under grace" with the personal testimony of the Roman Christians of "Grace"

i.e. the term "slaves" is a "human term"

We are to comply with our new nature, to yield.
There is a pragmatic reason for obeying..
"what fruit" did sin produce? Only death"
But God grants the "fruit" of sanctification ending in heaven

Paul goes from the Gentile illustration of the Slave to the Jewish illustration of the widow

Romans 7
1Or do you not know, brethren (for I am speaking to those who know the law), that the law has jurisdiction over a person as long as he lives?

she is bound to obey her husband

⁹knowing that Christ, having been raised from the dead, is never to die again; death no longer is master over Him.
¹⁰For the death that He died, He died to sin once for all; but the life that He lives, He lives to God.

Next.. an attitude follows. (v 11)
We see ourselves differently

Then there are actions :
- we resist sin's reign
- we present ourselves to God

¹¹Even so consider yourselves to be dead to sin, but alive to God in Christ Jesus.
¹²Therefore do not let sin reign in your mortal body so that you obey its lusts,
¹³and do not go on presenting the members of your body to sin as instruments of unrighteousness; but present yourselves to God as those alive from the dead, and your members as instruments of righteousness to God.
¹⁴For sin shall not be master over you, for you are not under law but under grace.

And there is an assurance (v 14)
Sin will not master us
because we have a new master -
we are "under Grace"

Another question is raised : -
"could we ever take advantage of grace ? "

The answer ? "No. We must obey our new master - grace . "

¹⁵What then? Shall we sin because we are not under law but under grace? May it never be!
¹⁶Do you not know that when you present yourselves to someone as slaves for obedience, you are slaves of the one whom you obey, either of sin resulting in death, or of obedience resulting in righteousness?
¹⁷But thanks be to God that though you were slaves of sin, you became obedient from the heart to that form of teaching to which you were committed, > i.e. entrusted
¹⁸and having been freed from sin, you became slaves of righteousness.

Paul supports the idea of being "under grace" with the personal testimony of the Roman Christians. i.e "Grace"

. the term "slaves" is a "human term"

We are to comply with our new nature, to yield .

There is a pragmatic reason for obeying.
"what fruit" did sin produce?
Only death"

But God grants the "fruit" of sanctification ending in heaven

¹⁹I am speaking in human terms because of the weakness of your flesh For just as you presented your members as slaves to impurity and to lawlessness, resulting in further lawlessness, so now present your members as slaves to righteousness, resulting in sanctification.
²⁰For when you were slaves of sin, you were free in regard to righteousness.
²¹Therefore what benefit were you then deriving from the things of which you are now ashamed? For the outcome of those things is death.
²²But now having been freed from sin and enslaved to God, you derive your benefit, resulting in sanctification, and the outcome, eternal life.
²³For the wages of sin is death, but the free gift of God is eternal life in Christ Jesus our Lord.

Paul goes from the Gentile illustration of the slave to the Jewish illustration of the widow

Romans 7
¹Or do you not know, brethren (for I am speaking to those who know the law), that the law has jurisdiction over a person as long as he lives?

she is bound to obey her husband

Conclusion:

¹⁷So now, no longer am I the one doing it, but (sin) which dwells in me.
¹⁸For I know that nothing good dwells in me, that is, in my (flesh) for the willing is present in me, but the doing of the good is not.
¹⁹For the good that I want, I do not do, but I practice the very evil that I do not want.
²⁰But if I am doing the very thing I do not want, I am no longer the one doing it, but sin which dwells in me.
²¹I find then the principle that evil is present in me, the one who wants to do good.
²²For I joyfully concur with the law of God in the inner man,
²³but I see a different law in the members of my (body) waging war against the law of my mind and making me a prisoner of the law of sin which is in my members.
²⁴Wretched man that I am! Who will set me free from the body of this death?
²⁵Thanks be to God through Jesus Christ our Lord! So then, on the one hand I myself with my mind am serving the law of God, but on the other, with my flesh the law of sin.

i.e. not my true nature but my 'flesh'

vv18-20 explains v17
   "It's not me but my sin"

Conclusion: "evil is present in me"

Paul is in a defeated position
He needs outside help

→ v 25 a is an involuntary verse of praise, parenthetical to the context anticipating ch.8

Security cont'd (ch.8)

Romans 8
¹Therefore there is now no condemnation for those who are in Christ Jesus.
²For the law of the Spirit of life in Christ Jesus has set you free from the law of sin and of death. the law demands judgment
³For what the Law could not do, weak as it was through the flesh, God did: sending His own Son in the likeness of sinful flesh and as an offering for sin, He condemned sin in the flesh,
⁴so that the requirement of the Law might be fulfilled in us, who do not walk according to the flesh but according to the Spirit.
⁵For those who are according to the flesh set their minds on the things of the flesh, but those who are according to the Spirit, the things of the Spirit.

We walk in the Spirit because we are of the Spirit. People live as people are.

① 1-4 a We are secure because we are delivered from the penalty of law

We are set free because God has met the law's demands

②
4b-11 We are secure because our salvation has already begun by the Holy Spirit

Paul has shown that whether as a non-Christian or even as a Christian he could not keep the law of God. His justification must come by God Grace..
   He now returns to the idea of our justification and security as from God

These are not commands but facts that necessarily accompany the save

⁶For the mind set on the flesh is death, but the mind set on the Spirit is life and peace,
⁷because the mind set on the flesh is hostile toward God; for it does not subject itself to the law of God, for it is not even able to do so,
⁸and those who are in the flesh cannot please God

The reason they live for the flesh is that they are dead to God.
   .. Hostile..
   ..rebellious..
   .. depraved..
   .. condemned..

The Spirit Grants us life now

... and will raise our bodies then

[9]However, you are not in the flesh but in the Spirit, if indeed the Spirit of God dwells in you But if anyone does not have the Spirit of Christ, he does not belong to Him.
[10]If Christ is in you, though the body is dead because of sin, yet (the spirit) is alive because of righteousness.
[11]But if the Spirit of Him who raised Jesus from the dead dwells in you, He who raised Christ Jesus from the dead will also give life to your (mortal bodies) through His Spirit who dwells in you.

The Christian has a totally different lifestyle..

..because of the Holy Spirit.
Not to have this life is not to have the Spirit .. and that is not to have God

(3) The Spirit's Rebirth has made us children of God.. thus heirs...
(12-17)

We must obey God..
because we are saved...

we live because we are shown to be sons,. family, because of our obedience!

and there is a sonship we experience in our souls

and like children we are the future certain recipients of all our heavenly Father's heritage

[12]So then, brethren, we are under obligation, not to the flesh, to live according to the flesh--
[13]for if you are living according to the flesh, you must die; but if by the Spirit you are putting to death the deeds of the body, you will live.
[14]For all who are being led by the Spirit of God, these are sons of God.
[15]For you have not received a spirit of slavery leading to fear again, but you have received a spirit of adoption as sons by which we cry out, "Abba! Father!"
[16]The Spirit Himself testifies with our spirit that we are children of God,
[17]and if children, heirs also, heirs of God and fellow heirs with Christ, if indeed we suffer with Him so that we may also be glorified with Him.

those who live continually in sin show their lost estate..
those who live by the Spirit's strength show their regenerate state

Paul explains "sons"... Those with a love of the Father..
..not slaves who obey out of begrudging fear

Before that time of entering our heritage we must suffer..
. and necessarily so..

(4) Our afflictions are not inconsistent with our sonship, only insignificant.

[18]For I consider that the sufferings of this present time are not worthy to be compared with the glory that is to be revealed to us.
[19]For the anxious longing of the creation waits eagerly for the revealing of the sons of God.

So Glorious is our salvation that the creation longs for our appearing that it might enter into it.

Why does the creation long for the appearing of the saints? It has been cursed, .. but in hope ..

Until then it suffers in hope of the birth of Life — the Kingdom —

In the same way we groan waiting for our resurrection

Our salvation is not fully experienced .. thus we must persevere ... and wait .. and pray.

& The Spirit helps us in our sojourn as He aids us in our prayers

The groaning of our prayer is understood by God and is in His will.

and His Sovereign will is good ..

"the image": our resurrection —

20For the creation was subjected to futility, not willingly, but because of Him who subjected it, in hope

21that the creation itself also will be set free from its slavery to corruption into the freedom of the glory of the children of God.

22For we know that the whole creation groans and suffers the pains of childbirth together until now.

23And not only this, but also we ourselves, having the first fruits of the Spirit, even we ourselves groan within ourselves, waiting eagerly for our adoption as sons, the redemption of our body.

24For in hope we have been saved, but hope that is seen is not hope; for who hopes for what he already sees?

25But if we hope for what we do not see, with perseverance we wait eagerly for it.

26In the same way the Spirit also helps our weakness; for we do not know how to pray as we should, but the Spirit Himself intercedes for us with groanings too deep for words;

27and He who searches the hearts knows what the mind of the Spirit is, because He intercedes for the saints according to the will of God.

28And we know that God causes all things to work together for good to those who love God, to those who are called according to His purpose.

29For those whom He foreknew, He also predestined to become conformed to the image of His Son, so that He would be the firstborn among many brethren;

30and these whom He predestined, He also called; and these whom He called, He also justified; and these whom He justified, He also glorified.

"groanings": the burden that the Spirit places on our heart ...

5 Our predestination sustains us His purpose to save us will not be thwarted

love → Predestination → calling → saving glorification

4 Christ's death and intercession for us is our security

If God gave the Greater, His Son, will He not give us all things?

31What then shall we say to these things? If God is for us, who is against us?

32He who did not spare His own Son, but delivered Him over for us all, how will He not also with Him freely give us all things?

There is no opposition

There is NO CONDEMNATION
Christ died for us and
mediates for us

There is no SEPARATION

Christians CAN suffer

We are unconquerable through Christ
as Nothing will separate us from
His love

[33]Who will bring a charge against God's elect?
God is the one who justifies;
[34]who is the one who condemns? Christ Jesus
is He who died, yes, rather who was raised,
who is at the right hand of God, who also
intercedes for us.
[35]Who will separate us from the love of
Christ? Will tribulation, or distress, or
persecution, or famine, or nakedness, or peril,
or sword?
[36]Just as it is written,
    "FOR YOUR SAKE WE ARE BEING
PUT TO DEATH ALL DAY LONG;
    WE WERE CONSIDERED AS SHEEP
TO BE SLAUGHTERED."
[37]But in all these things we overwhelmingly
conquer through Him who loved us.
[38]For I am convinced that neither death, nor
life, nor angels, nor principalities, nor things
present, nor things to come, nor powers,
[39]nor height, nor depth, nor any other created
thing, will be able to separate us from the love
of God, which is in Christ Jesus our Lord.

There is NO ACCUSATION.
GOD, The highest authority
  has justified us -

VII The Problem of Israel:
  The Vindication of God's Righteousness
  (Ch. 9-11)

ch.9 Israel's Past - Election
ch.10 Israel's Present - Rejection
ch.11 Israel's Future - Reception

In no way is Paul anti-Jewish
In no way does he feel God is
  finished with the nation

Romans 9
[1]I am telling the truth in Christ, I am not
lying, my conscience testifies with me in the
Holy Spirit,
[2]that I have great sorrow and unceasing grief
in my heart.
[3]For I could wish that I myself were accursed,
separated from Christ for the sake of my
brethren, my kinsmen according to the flesh,
[4]who are Israelites, to whom belongs the
adoption as sons, and the glory and the
covenants and the giving of the Law and the
temple service and the promises,
[5]whose are the fathers, and from whom is the
Christ according to the flesh, who is over all,
God blessed forever. Amen.

✡

Doctrinal	National	Practical
1 - 8	9 - 11	12 - 16

Israel's Past (ch. 9)

Because the nation has rejected Christ
has God's Word failed?

The true child of God is an "Isaac"
  - chosen and created of God

Another illustration: 2 boys, one
  womb . .

an unconditional election . . . .

[6]But it is not as though the word of God has
failed. For they are not all Israel who are
descended from Israel;
[7]nor are they all children because they are
Abraham's descendants, but: "THROUGH
ISAAC YOUR DESCENDANTS WILL BE
NAMED."
[8]That is, it is not the children of the flesh who
are children of God, but the children of the
promise are regarded as descendants.
[9]For this is the word of promise: "AT THIS
TIME I WILL COME, AND SARAH SHALL
HAVE A SON."
[10]And not only this, but there was Rebekah
also, when she had conceived twins by one
man, our father Isaac;
[11]for though the twins were not yet born and
had not done anything good or bad, so that
God's purpose according to His choice would
stand, not because of works but because of
Him who calls,

Being physically a Jew does not mean
  that you are spiritually God's child

¹²it was said to her, "THE OLDER WILL SERVE THE YOUNGER."
¹³Just as it is written, "JACOB I LOVED, BUT ESAU I HATED."

I.E.
"DID not show favor towArd"

¹⁴What shall we say then? There is no injustice with God, is there? May it never be!
¹⁵For He says to Moses, "I WILL HAVE MERCY ON WHOM I HAVE MERCY, AND I WILL HAVE COMPASSION ON WHOM I HAVE COMPASSION."
¹⁶So then it does not depend on the man who wills or the man who runs, but on God who has mercy.
¹⁷For the Scripture says to Pharaoh, "FOR THIS VERY PURPOSE I RAISED YOU UP, TO DEMONSTRATE MY POWER IN YOU, AND THAT MY NAME MIGHT BE PROCLAIMED THROUGHOUT THE WHOLE EARTH."

"Unjust! "

election is not built on justice but "mercy".

man's will and effort will not sAve - It is God's election

God can also harden any He is please to harden

¹⁸So then He has mercy on whom He desires, and He hardens whom He desires.
¹⁹You will say to me then, "Why does He still find fault? For who resists His will?"
²⁰On the contrary, who are you, O man, who answers back to God? The thing molded will not say to the molder, "Why did you make me like this," will it?
²¹Or does not the potter have a right over the clay, to make from the same lump one vessel for honorable use and another for common use?
²²What if God, although willing to demonstrate His wrath and to make His power known, endured with much patience vessels of wrath prepared for destruction?
²³And He did so to make known the riches of His glory upon vessels of mercy, which He prepared beforehand for glory,
²⁴even us, whom He also called, not from among Jews only, but also from among Gentiles.
²⁵As He says also in Hosea,
"I WILL CALL THOSE WHO WERE NOT MY PEOPLE, 'MY PEOPLE,'
AND HER WHO WAS NOT BELOVED, 'BELOVED.'"
²⁶"AND IT SHALL BE THAT IN THE PLACE WHERE IT WAS SAID TO THEM, 'YOU ARE NOT MY PEOPLE,'
THERE THEY SHALL BE CALLED SONS OF THE LIVING GOD."
²⁷Isaiah cries out concerning Israel, "THOUGH THE NUMBER OF THE SONS OF ISRAEL BE LIKE THE SAND OF THE SEA, IT IS THE REMNANT THAT WILL BE SAVED;
²⁸FOR THE LORD WILL EXECUTE HIS WORD ON THE EARTH, THOROUGHLY AND QUICKLY."

Conclusion: God is free to show mercy or hardness toward humanit
"So how can He declare Ascuilty?! "

man who is guilty, cannot answer back to a sovereign God.

middle Voice.. they did it.

Active voice.. the subject, God, DID it..
and He did so from eternity

He can make known His Power through Some and His mercy through others
He can sAve none
          some
          ANY
    or All   He is free over
even   a Guilty rAce
Gentiles

Isaiah agrees that being a Jew doesn't save.. It is mercy.. without which the nation would be destroyed.

of Judgment

²⁹And just as Isaiah foretold,
"UNLESS THE LORD OF SABAOTH
HAD LEFT TO US A POSTERITY,
WE WOULD HAVE BECOME LIKE
SODOM, AND WOULD HAVE RESEMBLED
GOMORRAH."

a saved remnant is an activity of God

conclusion:
There has been a strange turn of
events
- *Gentiles have been offered*
  a salvation they never sought

- *Israel in errant self-righteous-*
  ness has been hardened..

³⁰What shall we say then? That Gentiles, who
did not pursue righteousness, attained
righteousness, even the righteousness which
is by faith;
³¹but Israel, pursuing a law of righteousness,
did not arrive at that law.
³²Why? Because they did not pursue it by
faith, but as though it were by works. They
stumbled over the stumbling stone,
³³just as it is written,
"BEHOLD, I LAY IN ZION A STONE
OF STUMBLING AND A ROCK OF
OFFENSE,
AND HE WHO BELIEVES IN HIM
WILL NOT BE DISAPPOINTED."

* *because of their rejection of Christ*

ch. 10 explains...

Israel's Present (ch.10)
- why did Israel stumble?

Israel stumbled because of
a self righteous problem with
Justification by faith (vv 1-11)
And with the universal offer of
salvation (vv 12-21)

Romans 10
¹Brethren, my heart's desire and my prayer to
God for them is for their salvation.
²For I testify about them that they have a
zeal for God, but not in accordance with
knowledge.
³For not knowing about God's righteousness
and seeking to establish their own, they did
not subject themselves to the righteousness of
God.
⁴For Christ is the end of the law for
righteousness to everyone who believes.
⁵For Moses writes that the man who practices
the righteousness which is based on law shall
live by that righteousness.
⁶But the righteousness based on faith speaks
as follows: "DO NOT SAY IN YOUR HEART,
'WHO WILL ASCEND INTO HEAVEN?' (that
is, to bring Christ down),
⁷or 'WHO WILL DESCEND INTO THE
ABYSS?' (that is, to bring Christ up from the
dead)."
⁸But what does it say? "THE WORD IS NEAR
YOU, IN YOUR MOUTH AND IN YOUR
HEART"--that is, the word of faith which we
are preaching,
⁹that if you confess with your mouth Jesus as
Lord, and believe in your heart that God
raised Him from the dead, you will be saved;
¹⁰for with the heart a person believes,
resulting in righteousness, and with the
mouth he confesses, resulting in salvation.
¹¹For the Scripture says, "WHOEVER
BELIEVES IN HIM WILL NOT BE
DISAPPOINTED."
¹²For there is no distinction between Jew and
Greek; for the same Lord is Lord of all,
abounding in riches for all who call on Him;

Paul prays for Israel..
..because of their error

They were self righteous..
.. and Rebellious against God's
standard of righteousness..
which is Jesus Christ.

the end": The law is terminated as
a means of Righteousness. Because
of Jesus.

To be saved by law one must contin-
ually Do it

But to be saved by faith is to do
nothing because it has already
been done by Christ. (vv 6-10)

merely believe in the message of
what God has accomplished in
the perfect life, Death and
Resurrection of Jesus Christ...

..and confess it as true

"...ved" because we receive the
righteousness of God and His
salvation ..
..Just as the Bible says
in Isaiah

and this is available for
"whoever"....because God is the
God and Savior of all.

¹³for "WHOEVER WILL CALL ON THE NAME OF THE LORD WILL BE SAVED." ¹⁴How then will they call on Him in whom they have not believed? How will they believe in Him whom they have not heard? And how will they hear without a preacher? ¹⁵How will they preach unless they are sent? Just as it is written, "HOW BEAUTIFUL ARE THE FEET OF THOSE WHO BRING GOOD NEWS OF GOOD THINGS!"

¹⁶However, they did not all heed the good news; for Isaiah says, "LORD, WHO HAS BELIEVED OUR REPORT?" ¹⁷So faith comes from hearing, and hearing by the word of Christ. ¹⁸But I say, surely they have never heard, have they? Indeed they have;

"THEIR VOICE HAS GONE OUT INTO ALL THE EARTH,
AND THEIR WORDS TO THE ENDS OF THE WORLD."

¹⁹But I say, surely Israel did not know, did they? First Moses says,

"I WILL MAKE YOU JEALOUS BY THAT WHICH IS NOT A NATION,
BY A NATION WITHOUT UNDERSTANDING WILL I ANGER YOU."

²⁰And Isaiah is very bold and says,

"I WAS FOUND BY THOSE WHO DID NOT SEEK ME,
I BECAME MANIFEST TO THOSE WHO DID NOT ASK FOR ME."

²¹But as for Israel He says, "ALL THE DAY LONG I HAVE STRETCHED OUT MY HANDS TO A DISOBEDIENT AND OBSTINATE PEOPLE."

Israel's Future (ch. 11)

Romans 11

¹I say then, God has not rejected His people, has He? May it never be! For I too am an Israelite, a descendant of Abraham, of the tribe of Benjamin. ²God has not rejected His people whom He foreknew Or do you not know what the Scripture says in the passage about Elijah, how he pleads with God against Israel? ³"Lord, THEY HAVE KILLED YOUR PROPHETS, THEY HAVE TORN DOWN YOUR ALTARS, AND I ALONE AM LEFT, AND THEY ARE SEEKING MY LIFE." ⁴But what is the divine response to him? "I HAVE KEPT for Myself SEVEN THOUSAND MEN WHO HAVE NOT BOWED THE KNEE TO BAAL." ⁵In the same way then, there has also come to be at the present time a remnant according to God's gracious choice. ⁶But if it is by grace, it is no longer on the basis of works, otherwise grace is no longer grace.

Handwritten margin notes:

But have the nations indeed heard the message of salvation? Yes... as Ps.19 spoke

Is all of Israel Rejected? "No.. Paul is "exhibit A"

Just as in Elijah's day, God still has a remnant.

— As Joel said

Paul proves his point through Logic

The Gospel has been sent to all.. Just as Israel heard the wonderful message of redemption from the Babylonian captivity.

But Israel would Reject the gospel "report"

thus salvation comes through believing the message of Christ

general revelation anticipated the specific revelation of Christ

Did Israel know of Gentile salvation Moses prophesied of it,..

..as well as Isaiah..

But...
.. Israel's Rejection by God is not total (1-8)
nor is it final (9-32)

"sleep"...
Deadness to
All around
them

used in Ps.69 of David's enemies'
contempt of their king

Is God finished with them?
No!
The church's very salvation is to move
the Jew to jealousy

Anti-Semitism should never arise in
Christianity..."because our faith is Jewish

Don't let your doctrine of Grace produce
in you an irreverence for God.

"If" Faithfulness always indicates
true faith

7What then? What Israel is seeking, it has not obtained, but those who were chosen obtained it, and the rest were hardened;
8just as it is written,
"GOD GAVE THEM A SPIRIT OF STUPOR,
EYES TO SEE NOT AND EARS TO HEAR NOT,
DOWN TO THIS VERY DAY."
9And David says,
"LET THEIR TABLE BECOME A SNARE AND A TRAP,
AND A STUMBLING BLOCK AND A RETRIBUTION TO THEM.
10LET THEIR EYES BE DARKENED TO SEE NOT,
AND BEND THEIR BACKS FOREVER."

11I say then, they did not stumble so as to fall, did they? May it never be! But by their transgression salvation has come to the Gentiles, to make them jealous.
12Now if their transgression is riches for the world and their failure is riches for the Gentiles, how much more will their fulfillment be! - the Kingdom -
13But I am speaking to you who are Gentiles. Inasmuch then as I am an apostle of Gentiles, I magnify my ministry,
14if somehow I might move to jealousy my fellow countrymen and save some of them.
15For if their rejection is the reconciliation of the world, what will their acceptance be but life from the dead?
16If the first piece of dough is holy, the lump is also; and if the root is holy, the branches are too.
Abraham and the Covenant

17But if some of the branches were broken off, and you, being a wild olive, were grafted in among them and became partaker with them of the rich root of the olive tree,
18do not be arrogant toward the branches; but if you are arrogant, remember that it is not you who supports the root, but the root supports you.
19You will say then, "Branches were broken off so that I might be grafted in."
20Quite right, they were broken off for their unbelief, but you stand by your faith Do not be conceited, but fear;
21for if God did not spare the natural branches, He will not spare you, either.
22Behold then the kindness and severity of God; to those who fell, severity, but to you, God's kindness, if you continue in His kindness; otherwise you also will be cut off.
23And they also, if they do not continue in their unbelief, will be grafted in, for God is able to graft them in again.
24For if you were cut off from what is by nature a wild olive tree, and were grafted contrary to nature into a cultivated olive tree, how much more will these who are the natural branches be grafted into their own olive tree?

Conclusion: The nation as a whole
is in ignorance
and Judicial darkness

"their fulfillment.: When Israel
trusts their Savior

Paul's ministry always had Jews in
mind

He knew they had a future because the
world's new life in the Kingdom
rests on Israel's reception of Christ

Christians Partake of "the rich root".
..the blessing of Abraham's promised
seed, Christ

"But this was in God's purpose to
Replace them!"

True but this occurs through nothing
of us but only through grace

Jn.15:2; Col.1:23

But there will be a future for
the nation of Israel
If God can save us He can surely
Save them

"the mystery"
- Israel is darkened partially
- while the church is gathered
- and then all the nation will be saved

25For I do not want you, brethren, to be uninformed of this mystery--so that you will not be wise in your own estimation--that a partial hardening has happened to Israel until the fullness of the Gentiles has come in;
26and so all Israel will be saved; just as it is written,
"THE DELIVERER WILL COME FROM ZION,
HE WILL REMOVE UNGODLINESS FROM JACOB."
27"THIS IS MY COVENANT WITH THEM, WHEN I TAKE AWAY THEIR SINS."
28From the standpoint of the gospel they are enemies for your sake, but from the standpoint of God's choice they are beloved for the sake of the fathers;
29for the gifts and the calling of God are irrevocable.
30For just as you once were disobedient to God, but now have been shown mercy because of their disobedience,
31so these also now have been disobedient, that because of the mercy shown to you they also may now be shown mercy.
32For God has shut up all in disobedience so that He may show mercy to all.

... when Christ returns and judges Israel..

the reason for such divine faithfulness

Thus they are still seen as God's people

You were shown mercy..

. they will be shown mercy

Because all are undeserving, God can save any.

God's sovereign workings evoke worship from Paul

33Oh, the depth of the riches both of the wisdom and knowledge of God! How unsearchable are His judgments and unfathomable His ways!
34For WHO HAS KNOWN THE MIND OF THE LORD, OR WHO BECAME HIS COUNSELOR?
35Or WHO HAS FIRST GIVEN TO HIM THAT IT MIGHT BE PAID BACK TO HIM AGAIN?
36For from Him and through Him and to Him are all things To Him be the glory forever. Amen.

all may look evil but God has a plan
none know but Him

He is free from all men -
obligated to none

. as He is the source
means
purpose of all

VIII the Application of Righteousness
(Ch. 12 - 16)

1. First, our response to God.
Devotion because of this mercy
(12: 1-2)

Romans 12
1Therefore I urge you, brethren, by the mercies of God, to present your bodies a living and holy sacrifice, acceptable to God, which is your spiritual service of worship.
2And do not be conformed to this world, but be transformed by the renewing of your mind, so that you may prove what the will of God is, that which is good and acceptable and perfect.

The Command: "Present"

The Motivation : "mercies"

The Prevention : "the world"
The Result : "transformation"
The Process : "Renewing"

3For through the grace given to me I say to everyone among you not to think more highly of himself than he ought to think; but to think so as to have sound judgment, as God has allotted to each a measure of faith.

4For just as we have many members in one body and all the members do not have the same function,

5so we, who are many, are one body in Christ, and individually members one of another.

6Since we have gifts that differ according to the grace given to us, each of us is to exercise them accordingly: if prophecy, according to the proportion of his faith;

7if service, in his serving; or he who teaches, in his teaching;

8or he who exhorts, in his exhortation; he who gives, with liberality; he who leads, with diligence; he who shows mercy, with cheerfulness.

9Let love be without hypocrisy Abhor what is evil; cling to what is good.

10Be devoted to one another in brotherly love; give preference to one another in honor;

11not lagging behind in diligence, fervent in spirit, serving the Lord;

12rejoicing in hope, persevering in tribulation, devoted to prayer,

13contributing to the needs of the saints, practicing hospitality.

14Bless those who persecute you; bless and do not curse.

15Rejoice with those who rejoice, and weep with those who weep.

16Be of the same mind toward one another; do not be haughty in mind, but associate with the lowly Do not be wise in your own estimation.

17Never pay back evil for evil to anyone Respect what is right in the sight of all men.

18If possible, so far as it depends on you, be at peace with all men.

19Never take your own revenge, beloved, but leave room for the wrath of God, for it is written, "VENGEANCE IS MINE, I WILL REPAY," says the Lord.

20"BUT IF YOUR ENEMY IS HUNGRY, FEED HIM, AND IF HE IS THIRSTY, GIVE HIM A DRINK; FOR IN SO DOING YOU WILL HEAP BURNING COALS ON HIS HEAD."

21Do not be overcome by evil, but overcome evil with good.

2. The Church (3-16)

- Be humble

- Be responsible

- Be loving

3. Our Enemies (17-21)

Romans 13

¹Every person is to be in subjection to the governing authorities For there is no authority except from God, and those which exist are established by God.

²Therefore whoever resists authority has opposed the ordinance of God; and they who have opposed will receive condemnation upon themselves.

³For rulers are not a cause of fear for good behavior, but for evil. Do you want to have no fear of authority? Do what is good and you will have praise from the same;

⁴for it is a minister of God to you for good. But if you do what is evil, be afraid; for it does not bear the sword for nothing; for it is a minister of God, an avenger who brings wrath on the one who practices evil.

⁵Therefore it is necessary to be in subjection, not only because of wrath, but also for conscience' sake.

⁶For because of this you also pay taxes, for rulers are servants of God, devoting themselves to this very thing.

⁷Render to all what is due them: tax to whom tax is due; custom to whom custom; fear to whom fear; honor to whom honor.

⁸Owe nothing to anyone except to love one another; for he who loves his neighbor has fulfilled the law.

⁹For this, "YOU SHALL NOT COMMIT ADULTERY, YOU SHALL NOT MURDER, YOU SHALL NOT STEAL, YOU SHALL NOT COVET," and if there is any other commandment, it is summed up in this saying, "YOU SHALL LOVE YOUR NEIGHBOR AS YOURSELF."

¹⁰Love does no wrong to a neighbor; therefore love is the fulfillment of the law.

¹¹Do this, knowing the time, that it is already the hour for you to awaken from sleep; for now salvation is nearer to us than when we believed.

¹²The night is almost gone, and the day is near Therefore let us lay aside the deeds of darkness and put on the armor of light.

¹³Let us behave properly as in the day, not in carousing and drunkenness, not in sexual promiscuity and sensuality, not in strife and jealousy.

¹⁴But put on the Lord Jesus Christ, and make no provision for the flesh in regard to its lusts.

---

4. The Government (13:1-7)

Be a model citizen ..
.. as government is from God

To rebel will bring punishment

.. as government is God's ordained sword

We obey not just out of fear but because of conscience

.. because government is a divine servant

5. Our Neighbors
- love him

- win him

- be distinct from him

- model for him
- beware however of the world temptations

Romans 14

¹Now accept the one who is weak in faith, but not for the purpose of passing judgment on his opinions.

²One person has faith that he may eat all things, but he who is weak eats vegetables only.

³The one who eats is not to regard with contempt the one who does not eat, and the one who does not eat is not to judge the one who eats, for God has accepted him.

⁴Who are you to judge the servant of another? To his own master he stands or falls; and he will stand, for the Lord is able to make him stand.

⁵One person regards one day above another, another regards every day alike Each person must be fully convinced in his own mind.

⁶He who observes the day, observes it for the Lord, and he who eats, does so for the Lord, for he gives thanks to God; and he who eats not, for the Lord he does not eat, and gives thanks to God.

⁷For not one of us lives for himself, and not one dies for himself;

⁸for if we live, we live for the Lord, or if we die, we die for the Lord; therefore whether we live or die, we are the Lord's.

⁹For to this end Christ died and lived again, that He might be Lord both of the dead and of the living.

¹⁰But you, why do you judge your brother? Or you again, why do you regard your brother with contempt? For we will all stand before the judgment seat of God.

¹¹For it is written,
"AS I LIVE, SAYS THE LORD, EVERY KNEE SHALL BOW TO ME,
AND EVERY TONGUE SHALL GIVE PRAISE TO GOD."

¹²So then each one of us will give an account of himself to God.

¹³Therefore let us not judge one another anymore, but rather determine this--not to put an obstacle or a stumbling block in a brother's way.

¹⁴I know and am convinced in the Lord Jesus that nothing is unclean in itself; but to him who thinks anything to be unclean, to him it is unclean.

¹⁵For if because of food your brother is hurt, you are no longer walking according to love Do not destroy with your food him for whom Christ died.

¹⁶Therefore do not let what is for you a good thing be spoken of as evil;

¹⁷for the kingdom of God is not eating and drinking, but righteousness and peace and joy in the Holy Spirit.

---

6 Unity In Cultural Areas
(Ch.14 - 15:13)

- food

ⓐ "Live and let live"

ⓑ let God judge them, not you..

- days

..as
ⓒ all things are done to God's glory
  - in life and death

we are the first of a totally submitted universe

ⓓ But be sensitive to an abuse of freedom

18For he who in this way serves Christ is acceptable to God and approved by men.
19So then we pursue the things which make for peace and the building up of one another.
20Do not tear down the work of God for the sake of food All things indeed are clean, but they are evil for the man who eats and gives offense.
21It is good not to eat meat or to drink wine, or to do anything by which your brother stumbles.
22The faith which you have, have as your own conviction before God. Happy is he who does not condemn himself in what he approves.
23But he who doubts is condemned if he eats, because his eating is not from faith; and whatever is not from faith is sin.

Romans 15
1Now we who are strong ought to bear the weaknesses of those without strength and not just please ourselves.
2Each of us is to please his neighbor for his good, to his edification.
3For even Christ did not please Himself; but as it is written, "THE REPROACHES OF THOSE WHO REPROACHED YOU FELL ON ME."
4For whatever was written in earlier times was written for our instruction, so that through perseverance and the encouragement of the Scriptures we might have hope.
5Now may the God who gives perseverance and encouragement grant you to be of the same mind with one another according to Christ Jesus,
6so that with one accord you may with one voice glorify the God and Father of our Lord Jesus Christ.
7Therefore, accept one another, just as Christ also accepted us to the glory of God.
8For I say that Christ has become a servant to the circumcision on behalf of the truth of God to confirm the promises given to the fathers,
9and for the Gentiles to glorify God for His mercy; as it is written,
"THEREFORE I WILL GIVE PRAISE TO YOU AMONG THE GENTILES,
AND I WILL SING TO YOUR NAME."
10Again he says,
"REJOICE, O GENTILES, WITH HIS PEOPLE."
11And again,
"PRAISE THE LORD ALL YOU GENTILES,
AND LET ALL THE PEOPLES PRAISE HIM."

e. Make the glory of God your aim

f. Be like Jesus

Paul prays for their unity

.. as it glorifies God..

.. and exemplifies Christ.

He united Jew and Gentile into one body and accepts both..

¹²Again Isaiah says,
"THERE SHALL COME THE ROOT OF JESSE,
AND HE WHO ARISES TO RULE OVER THE GENTILES,
IN HIM SHALL THE GENTILES HOPE."
¹³Now may the God of hope fill you with all joy and peace in believing, so that you will abound in hope by the power of the Holy Spirit.

this kind of unity brings Joy, peace and assurance or hope...

¹⁴And concerning you, my brethren, I myself also am convinced that you yourselves are full of goodness, filled with all knowledge and able also to admonish one another.
¹⁵But I have written very boldly to you on some points so as to remind you again, because of the grace that was given me from God,
¹⁶to be a minister of Christ Jesus to the Gentiles, ministering as a priest the gospel of God, so that my offering of the Gentiles may become acceptable, sanctified by the Holy Spirit.
¹⁷Therefore in Christ Jesus I have found reason for boasting in things pertaining to God.
¹⁸For I will not presume to speak of anything except what Christ has accomplished through me, resulting in the obedience of the Gentiles by word and deed,
¹⁹in the power of signs and wonders, in the power of the Spirit; so that from Jerusalem and round about as far as Illyricum I have fully preached the gospel of Christ.
²⁰And thus I aspired to preach the gospel, not where Christ was already named, so that I would not build on another man's foundation;
²¹but as it is written,
"THEY WHO HAD NO NEWS OF HIM SHALL SEE,
AND THEY WHO HAVE NOT HEARD SHALL UNDERSTAND."
²²For this reason I have often been prevented from coming to you;
²³but now, with no further place for me in these regions, and since I have had for many years a longing to come to you
²⁴whenever I go to Spain--for I hope to see you in passing, and to be helped on my way there by you, when I have first enjoyed your company for a while--
²⁵but now, I am going to Jerusalem serving the saints.
²⁶For Macedonia and Achaia have been pleased to make a contribution for the poor among the saints in Jerusalem.
²⁷Yes, they were pleased to do so, and they are indebted to them. For if the Gentiles have shared in their spiritual things, they are indebted to minister to them also in material things.
²⁸Therefore, when I have finished this, and have put my seal on this fruit of theirs, I will go on by way of you to Spain.
²⁹I know that when I come to you, I will come in the fullness of the blessing of Christ.

men believe and continue only because of God's Grace

7- Missions

"you are obeying well "

"I wrote only to remind you".

".. because I am a priest and you are my offering "

But successful ministry comes by the power of the Holy Spirit through Christ's headship

Paul can do NOTHING apart from Christ

and Paul feels a responsibility to all the world..

.. as this was the purpose of Messiah

God's will for Paul is missions

and the local church has the responsibility to fund missions...

.. and to aid suffering Jewish brethren

having done all required

³⁰Now I urge you, brethren, by our Lord Jesus Christ and by the love of the Spirit, to strive together with me in your prayers to God for me,

³¹that I may be rescued from those who are disobedient in Judea, and that my service for Jerusalem may prove acceptable to the saints;

³²so that I may come to you in joy by the will of God and find refreshing rest in your company.

³³Now the God of peace be with you all. Amen.

and the power of God is invoked by prayer

God can control the evil ..

.. and the good ..

.. and grant success to the minister

Romans 16

¹I commend to you our sister Phoebe, who is a servant of the church which is at Cenchrea;

²that you receive her in the Lord in a manner worthy of the saints, and that you help her in whatever matter she may have need of you; for she herself has also been a helper of many, and of myself as well.

³Greet Prisca and Aquila, my fellow workers in Christ Jesus,

⁴who for my life risked their own necks, to whom not only do I give thanks, but also all the churches of the Gentiles;

⁵also greet the church that is in their house Greet Epaenetus, my beloved, who is the first convert to Christ from Asia.

⁶Greet Mary, who has worked hard for you.

⁷Greet Andronicus and Junias, my kinsmen and my fellow prisoners, who are outstanding among the apostles, who also were in Christ before me.

⁸Greet Ampliatus, my beloved in the Lord.

⁹Greet Urbanus, our fellow worker in Christ, and Stachys my beloved.

¹⁰Greet Apelles, the approved in Christ. Greet those who are of the household of Aristobulus.

¹¹Greet Herodion, my kinsman. Greet those of the household of Narcissus, who are in the Lord.

¹²Greet Tryphaena and Tryphosa, workers in the Lord. Greet Persis the beloved, who has worked hard in the Lord.

¹³Greet Rufus, a choice man in the Lord, also his mother and mine.

¹⁴Greet Asyncritus, Phlegon, Hermes, Patrobas, Hermas and the brethren with them.

¹⁵Greet Philologus and Julia, Nereus and his sister, and Olympas, and all the saints who are with them.

¹⁶Greet one another with a holy kiss. All the churches of Christ greet you.

Paul looks at the common people who serve in the ministry

• a woman

• a couple

• someone geographically distinct

• Paul's mentors

• slaves

• those totally culturally opposite from us

• the elderly
• twins?
• the Great

• the common

Paul's secretary

[17]Now I urge you, brethren, keep your eye on those who cause dissensions and hindrances contrary to the teaching which you learned, and turn away from them.
[18]For such men are slaves, not of our Lord Christ but of their own appetites; and by their smooth and flattering speech they deceive the hearts of the unsuspecting.
[19]For the report of your obedience has reached to all; therefore I am rejoicing over you, but I want you to be wise in what is good and innocent in what is evil.
[20]The God of peace will soon crush Satan under your feet The grace of our Lord Jesus be with you.
[21]Timothy my fellow worker greets you, and so do Lucius and Jason and Sosipater, my kinsmen.
[22]I, Tertius, who write this letter, greet you in the Lord.
[23]Gaius, host to me and to the whole church, greets you Erastus, the city treasurer greets you, and Quartus, the brother.
[24][The grace of our Lord Jesus Christ be with you all. Amen.]
[25]Now to Him who is able to establish you according to my gospel and the preaching of Jesus Christ, according to the revelation of the mystery which has been kept secret for long ages past,
[26]but now is manifested, and by the Scriptures of the prophets, according to the commandment of the eternal God, has been made known to all the nations, leading to obedience of faith;
[27]to the only wise God, through Jesus Christ, be the glory forever. Amen.

How about those who reject Christian truth
- beware
- turn away
- identify
- fear them

- they are of Satan

Conclusion:
The Gospel can "establish" a man...
..as Paul's words
  are Christ's words
  are God's words   Thus..
..the gospel is commanded
..to all the nations..

to the Glory of God
  through Jesus Christ